The Arctic Sonata
The Courage To Rise

Foreword by Grammy-Nominated, Platinum-Selling Pianist and Composer David Lanz

Maureen Girard

Published by Franklin Publishers
Printed in the United States of America

For permissions, inquiries, or additional copies, contact:
Franklin Publishers
www.franklinpublishers.com

Foreward

I met Maureen in her lovely Whidbey Island piano studio more than a decade or so ago after she had contacted me to give a piano workshop for her students. It would be the first of several very successful events and concerts organized by Maureen for her students and her community.

She was very focused and had created a supportive, encouraging, and nurturing environment for her many students. I have given countless workshops for teachers and their students over the years, and her's were among the most prepared and talented group I've ever encountered.

Her love of music and her musicianship was embedded into the hearts and hands of her students. Her story is a reflection of life challenges met with an artistic soul. Bravo!

David Lanz

www.davidlanz.com

David Lanz
Grammy-Nominated, Platinum-Selling Pianist and Composer

Acknowledgments

To my parents, Bill and Claire Lynch, who did their best to love and raise their family under extraordinarily difficult circumstances. To my uncle, Eddie Lynch, and to all of my family, thank you for your love. To my daughter and my grandson, Tu: I love you with all my heart. You, too, will find the **Courage to Rise**.

To Professor Martin Behnke at Willamette University, for giving me the opportunity of a lifetime and that changed my life forever.

To my more than 1,200 piano students and their families: Being your piano teacher has been one of the greatest joys of my life.

To the Support Team at Apple: your help has been invaluable.

To my brother, William O'Sullivan Lynch—"Billy" (July 20, 1946 - August 24, 1997). I used to sneak into your room to look at your sketches and artwork. From an early age, you showed me that Art is Important.

And finally, to Ray Barner, a retired U.S. Marine, who took me out of harm's way when I could not save or protect myself... and who's been by my side ever since. You're my hero.

Table of Contents

Introduction

Curtains Rise – A Legacy of Music and Showbiz

It wasn't me who chose music—it was music that chose me. There was no other path I could take. I followed my calling to become a professional pianist and singer, starting with nothing and risking everything. Our once-thriving family had crumbled, and for a time, I had no piano and no one actively guiding me. Yet, I can't truly say I had nothing—because I had music.

It was my inheritance from my beloved uncle, Eddie Lynch. Music coursed through my veins as surely as it did through his. It was more than a passion; it was a legacy—an unbreakable thread that tied us together. From his influence, I came to realize that music would become my destiny—just as it had been his. It was in my blood, shaping my path and calling me forward, just as it had shaped his extraordinary life in show business.

Eddie was my guiding star. He began his career as a singer and dancer during the Great Depression, a time when talent often meant the difference between survival and obscurity.

Starting in vaudeville at a young age, Eddie's talent shone so brightly that he caught the attention of one of the most famous and highest-paid entertainers of his time—Al Jolson. Recognizing Eddie's potential, Jolson took him under his wing, mentoring him and giving him his start in New York's vibrant show business scene.

Over time, Eddie's career evolved. He wore many hats—choreographer, producer, and ultimately, stage manager of the iconic Circus Maximus showroom at Caesars Palace in Las Vegas.

Eddie saw my love for music early on and nurtured it in the way only he could. He began taking me backstage with him while working burlesque shows in Atlantic City. My seat was always behind the heavy velvet curtains, where I could watch the opening acts—usually comedic former vaudevillians. Their jokes went over my head, but the thrill of being backstage, surrounded by the buzz of performers and stagehands, was exhilarating. When the showgirls appeared, someone would gently escort me out. I wasn't allowed to watch their performances, but I caught glimpses of them backstage—draped in sequins and pearls, towering in high heels, with feathers cascading from elaborate headdresses. Those fleeting moments felt like a glimpse into another world, one I knew I wasn't yet old enough to fully understand.

Those early experiences left an indelible mark on me. They planted the seeds for a future I couldn't yet imagine—one where I would not only perform as a pianist and singer but also produce shows of my own. Eddie's world became my inspiration, shaping both my vision for music and performance and my understanding of who I was meant to be.

Growing up in the vibrant New York metropolitan area, life was full of music, family, and the kind of resilience that would define my path. My parents, Claire and Bill, navigated their own challenges, and our lives echoed with stories of hope, perseverance, and love. It was here that my passion for music took root—a passion that would one day carry me to places beyond my wildest imagination.

I still feel Eddie watching over me, his warm smile ever present—especially in my 88Keys Piano Studio and Performance Space, where his picture hung as a silent reminder of where it all began. In that cherished space, I taught over a thousand piano students and produced unforgettable house concerts for more than a decade. Each day, as I walked past his picture, I'd smile back, reflecting on my journey—from losing my beloved piano and having none at all to owning three beautiful grand pianos.

I know he'd be proud, seeing his legacy live on through me—forever bound by our shared love of music and its ability to transform lives.

This is my story.

Unexpected News

"Hi honey, I'm home!" My dad, Bill, called out as he stepped into their cozy Bronx brownstone apartment, the smell of dinner wafting from the kitchen.

"Welcome home, Bill," my mom, Claire, replied, apron tied neatly at her waist as she peeked out from the kitchen doorway. "The kids are asleep...dinner's ready... and I've got some big news." "Big news?" my dad said, hanging up his coat and settling into his favorite chair. "Well, let's see—did we hit the jackpot? ...Or maybe we're moving to Park Avenue?" He said, with a smirk as he loosened his tie.

"Not quite, Bill." My mom entered the room, smoothing her dress and clutching a towel.

Her voice dropped just slightly, a hint of anticipation in her tone. "I went to the doctor today."

"Is everything OK? ...You're healthy as a horse, right?" He leaned back, grinning, fully expecting to be met with reassurance.

"Well...I'm healthy as a horse alright...one who's pregnant, Bill. "She blurted it out, standing tall as if bracing for the fallout.

There was a beat of silence, and then my dad sprang forward, nearly choking on his own disbelief. "You're *what?* ..Claire... is this a joke? ... We've already got two kids! We're done, remember? Finito! Kaput! How—"

"Oh, Bill." ...My mom's voice cut in, firm but playful, her expression almost daring him to keep going. "It's not like I did this all by myself."

I could imagine my dad throwing his hands up like Ralph Kramden in a classic Honeymooners moment and pacing the small living room, gesturing wildly. "I mean, Claire, we're not spring chickens! I'm already workin' double-time to keep food on the table, and now we've got a third mouth to feed?" "Well, what do you want me to do about it, Ralph—I mean, Bill?" my mom asked with a grin.

My mom, Claire, was 42, and my dad, Bill, was 48. Breaking the news to my dad about her pregnancy probably played out like a scene from The Honeymooners, the wildly popular TV show at the time. Jackie Gleason, the star of the show, was even one of my dad's customers.

Much like Ralph Kramden's exaggerated antics, my dad may have reacted with a mix of shock and humor. I can imagine him delivering a line straight from Ralph's playbook: "Well, here's another fine mess you've gotten us into. You're a riot, Claire. A regular riot..."

Claire was born in Montreal and was working as a model when she met my dad, who sold Cadillacs in Manhattan, across the street from the Ed Sullivan Theater, where his brother Eddie worked backstage. My mom's elegance and charm complemented my dad's charisma. Soon, I would join an older brother, nine years my senior, and a sister, seven years older. Our growing family prompted a move to a larger home in Yonkers, a city that borders the Bronx..right off of Park Avenue...in Yonkers... to a beautiful four-story house with three bedrooms. There, they became home owners for the first and only time in their lives.

I was born at Yonkers General Hospital on January 15, during an episode of "The Ed Sullivan Show," another family favorite. My dad's connection with Eddie brought him a steady stream of celebrities and show business customers who all wanted a new Cadillac every year. Ed Sullivan himself, was also a customer. It was a great arrangement for them. Eddie made his friends happy, and my dad made money.

Eddie and my dad were separated for a while during their childhood due to the Great Depression. Their mom sent my dad upstate to live on a farm while Eddie stayed with her in Brooklyn, selling bootleg liquor that she made in her bathtub.

By the time our family moved to Yonkers, the brothers had become reunited. They had really missed each other and were so happy to be together again. They were both naturally very funny. Their reunion as adults brought laughter and joy to our family gatherings around our dining room table.

If we didn't have company, my brother and, my sister and I would have dinner together in our kitchen nook. Our mom would make dinner for us and then she'd eat later with our dad after he got home from work.

Our kitchen nook became the setting for many childhood memories. The cozy corner had built-in benches around a small table that overlooked our backyard. Our brother Billy's antics often stole the show. He loved to make us laugh. He'd bring his ant farm and his live pet collection to dinner. He kept them in little boxes that had holes in them so that they could breathe. He had frogs, lizards, snakes, weird bugs, and even an electric eel—he'd pull something out, saying, "hey, look at this guy!" and elicit screams and laughter. Once, we had a baby alligator living in the bathtub.

Summers were spent picking peaches and pears from our backyard trees and helping our Mom can them in the basement. The fragrant jars lined the shelves under the stairs, their sweetness lasting all year.

My favorite spot in the basement was where the dark mahogany piano stood, tucked near the warmth of the furnace. From the moment I saw it, I fell in love. I asked my mom if it could be mine, and with a gentle smile, she said, "Yes, honey, it's yours." That simple moment sparked my lifelong love for the piano, and for music.

At six, I started piano lessons at Mr. Polar's music store on Warburton Avenue, a few miles from our house. A picture of him performing at Carnegie Hall hung on the wall by his studio, inspiring me. From that moment, I envisioned myself dressed in a gown, performing under the spotlight. I never doubted that dream.

Performing came naturally to me. When our parents hosted dinner parties, my mom would nudge me into the dining room to entertain guests. I'd sing and dance to "Calcutta," her favorite song that I'd learned from listening to "The Lawerence Welk Show." I'd make my way around the dining room table and into the living room, where the guests sat enjoying their cocktails. I'd do a few other numbers and then close with my comedic rendition of "I'm Looking Over My Dead Dog Rover," moving my arms around in a circular motion like a locomotive as I faded out of view. Then I'd come back and take a bow. The applause fueled my passion for entertaining. My Uncle Eddie, a vaudeville performer turned producer and director, recognized my love for music. He often took me backstage with him at performances, fostering my bond with him and the world of music and entertainment. When he visited, I'd stage basement performances using Mom's sheets as curtains and my piano for impromptu recitals. Eddie's laughter and encouragement made those moments unforgettable.

Picture of our mom working as a model crossing the street on
Broadway in Manhattan
photo courtesy of Lynch Family Photos circa late 1940s

Our mom was what was known as a photographer's model. The photographer that she worked for used pictures of her to show the quality of his work to potential clients. She was a stunning woman who laughed easily and who had a natural gracefulness about her. I adored her.

Life in Yonkers revolved around hills—our street, Hill Bright Terrace, lived up to its name. Winters brought sledding adventures, though one ended with a painful trip to the ER after I ran over my pinky finger. The memory of blood soaking through my glove and the dangling tip of my finger haunted me, but thanks to Mom's quick action, the hospital reattached it. The scar remains a testament to her care and my resilience. From that day on, building snowmen and forts replaced going sledding in my winter activities.

I started first grade at Sacred Heart, where my older brother and sister also went. I loved it. It gave us an excellent high, quality education, and I loved our uniforms. The girls wore crisp white button-down shirts with short sleeves, a green cardigan sweater with pockets in just the right places, green knee socks, and plaid jumpers. The boys dressed like little businessmen. They wore grey slacks with green suit jackets and ties. We all got the message that going to school and getting an education was not something that you did while wearing your street clothes.

Catholic school was where we learned how to be good students, good citizens and how to stay out of trouble. You did not want to get into trouble with the nuns. They had very effective ways of handling kids who weren't doing their work or measuring up to their high standards.

They had fear tactics—pointer stick slapped on desks—kids sent to the principal's office left lasting impressions. We came to school one day and saw that the nun had built a wall out of cut-up cardboard boxes that she'd taped together. It went from the floor to the ceiling. She moved the desks of the kids who she felt weren't "measuring up" behind the cardboard wall. I didn't know what to think when I came into our classroom that day. I just sat down at my desk. The nun gave us our work to do and then occasionally made a few trips to go behind the wall. This went on for a few weeks. Sometimes, we'd see a kid from behind the wall get escorted out to the hallway, and sometimes we never saw that kid again.

I sat next to a kid named Christopher. He was the most perfect-looking kid that you could imagine. He looked like he worked on Wall Street. He always got straight A's and A+'s. I made him my competition. I really wanted to outdo him in something...anything, just once. But it was impossible. He was the kid who'd bring the nun a shiny red apple and who was what is commonly known as the "teacher's pet." I kept trying to outdo him, but it never happened. My efforts to try and outdo him did however, make me become a better student.

Sacred Heart instilled in me the value of hard work and perseverance. My love for learning, nurtured by the encouragement of my family and teachers, fueled my determination to achieve my dreams. Growing up in the vibrant NY metropolitan area, surrounded by music, laughter, and love, provided the foundation for everything I aspired to become.

New York was more than a place; it was a symbol of excellence. As New Yorkers, we were expected to strive for greatness in everything we did. "Always do your best" wasn't just advice—it was the standard we lived by. We took immense pride in our first responders, who were our everyday heroes, and we carried ourselves with the pride and resilience that New York represented. To be from New York City was to embody the drive, strength, and ambition that defined the city itself.

A Childhood of Music and Memories

Our dining room had a swinging door that led to a big kitchen. The kitchen had a cozy nook, a shiny black-and-white hand-tiled counter, a spacious walk-in pantry, and a small bathroom where Mom "put her face on" every day. Next to that bathroom was a half door with a spring, which could be swung open. This door led to a landing three steps down. From there, you could either go through a door to an outside stairway leading to the driveway or turn right and descend a set of stairs to the basement—to my favorite place - where my piano awaited.

During this time, eating meat on Friday was considered a mortal sin in the Catholic religion. A MORTAL sin. Even if it was accidental, it meant eternal damnation in hell. I lived in quiet fear that my mom, who made our lunches, might one day mistakenly give me a bologna sandwich instead of peanut butter and jelly on a Friday. The thought really scared me.

The Church changed the rule during my third-grade year. What a relief! Eating meat on Fridays became a venial sin instead of a mortal one.

That meant you wouldn't be doomed to hell but would go to Purgatory, an in-between place, before eventually getting into heaven?

But I had questions—big ones. What about the people already burning in hell for eating meat on Fridays? Would they be moved to Purgatory? Or would they be allowed into heaven? How was this going to work? Questioning anything in the Catholic Church was not encouraged, especially during catechism class. But I raised my hand anyway and dared to ask my question. The nun glared at me, her face puffing up like a blowfish. "We don't ASK questions!" she snapped. I lowered my hand and tried to disappear into my seat. Even at that young age, I knew her answer didn't make sense. You couldn't just change something like that and not explain it.

That day, when I got home, I went straight to my piano, as I often did. But this time, it brought me more comfort than ever. I took solace in knowing that middle C would always be in the middle...no one would ever come along one day and tell me that they'd moved it. The music made sense. The low notes were on the bottom, the middle notes in the center, and the high notes at the top. It was logical, beautiful, and filled with joy—a world I could explore and had fallen in love with.

Sacred Heart had summer camps, and between our camp trips, our family outings, and our Brownie troop adventures, we explored Yonkers and countless iconic places in the New York metropolitan area. The NY City comprises five boroughs—Manhattan, Queens, Brooklyn, Staten Island, and the Bronx. Yonkers borders the Bronx, and is part of the metropolitan area.

Our family were regulars at the Bronx Zoo, the Botanical Gardens, and the Museum of Natural History. Of all these places, the Museum of Natural History was my favorite. My brother liked to call it the Museum of Natural Hysteria. The exhibits felt so real, with wax figures of people from various cultures, including Native Americans in canoes and Eskimos demonstrating their ways of life. Never in my wildest dreams could I ever have imagined standing next to real Eskimos one day—but that day would come.

The museum had a long wall depicting the timeline of human evolution, with glass cases displaying skulls and primitive tools. My favorite part was the dinosaur exhibit. The dinosaur skeletons were their actual size, towering above us in an enormous room that was so big that voices from people across the room traveled in echoes across it. Seeing life-sized woolly mammoths, complete with their wool and horns and flying dinosaurs hanging from the ceiling, was awe-inspiring.

The Hayden Planetarium was another magical place. We learned about the planets, the solar system, and the history of the universe. We watched space shows and walked a winding pathway going through the timeline of the universe, from when it began and learning about humanity's brief existence in it. It was incredible.

Another impactful visit was to Ellis Island. Touring the Statue of Liberty and Ellis Island left a lifelong impression. One of the most unforgettable experiences was climbing the long spiral staircase inside the Statue with my Brownie troop. Past "the point of no return," we climbed all the way to the crown. It was dark, humid, and crowded, with built-in resting seats for those who needed them. When we finally reached the top, we looked out of the crown. There was zero visibility outside, which meant that we could only see clouds through the windows—but it was extraordinary and exhilarating to be there.

We also toured the United Nations, went to the Empire State Building, attended a Yankees game, and soaked in the energy of the city.

The 1960s were transformative. We lived at the center of a musical revolution sparked by the Beatles, the Rolling Stones, and the great Black Motown singers and entertainers. The Ed Sullivan Show introduced them to us, broadcasting from Manhattan's Ed Sullivan Theater, less than twenty miles away. The energy swept over us like a wave, changing everything. I sat transfixed, watching these musicians, especially Diana Ross and the Supremes.

Diana Ross became my idol. She was the most beautiful woman that I'd ever seen.. and when she sang, it felt like she was singing right to me, a little kid sitting crossed-legged on the living room floor. My mouth would just drop open in sheer amazement and joy. My excitement and love for her has never changed.

One of the biggest highlights was the 1964–1965 New York World's Fair in Queens. We visited several times, and it was life-changing. The fair featured the iconic 140-foot-tall Unisphere, symbolizing "Peace Through Understanding." Acres of futuristic exhibits showcased innovations like video telephones and cars of tomorrow. We rode through buildings on guided rides with narrated recordings, marveling at the possibilities of the future. It was an extraordinary time, full of excitement and promise for an exciting future.

The Day the Music Stopped

Our lives began to change in the early 1960s when Dad started having problems with his voice. He was a smoker, and his ability to make a living depended on using his voice to sell Cadillacs for General Motors. Despite the doctors' warnings to quit smoking, he didn't stop, continuing to strain his voice as he worked.

Eventually, he had to undergo a series of operations. He would be home from work for weeks at a time, unable to speak, writing down what he wanted to say. By the time he finally quit smoking, it was too late. After his last surgery, part of his larynx was removed, leaving him barely able to speak above a whisper. The doctor told Mom he likely had only six months to live. At the time, it was common practice to tell such a diagnosis to the family, not the patient. Mom decided not to tell him. Instead, she suggested that we move to Las Vegas to be close to his brother, Uncle Eddie, knowing he would help us.

I'll never forget the day that changed my life forever. The noise was deafening—a chaotic, crashing racket. My upright piano, with its ivory keys and wood polished to a shine, had been my whole world. After school, I'd toss my book bag aside and rush down to play. But that day, as I descended the basement stairs, I stopped short, frozen in shock.

I saw my brother and his friends smashing my beloved piano into pieces with sledgehammers. The clanging of metal and splintering of wood echoed around me. All that remained was the gold plate that had held the strings. My world shattered alongside the piano. I don't remember the days immediately after or any mention of it in our house.

Mom had no experience managing finances or doing household chores. She grew up in a wealthy family in Quebec, where maids, butlers, and seamstresses handled all of the domestic tasks. As a result, she never learned any household skills herself. She loved fashion had been modeling in New York when she met Dad. After learning of his terminal diagnosis, medical expenses piled up, and money was running out. Our parents decided to sell our house in New York and move to Las Vegas to be near Uncle Eddie.

My mom found some buyers for the house. The new owners wanted the piano removed before they moved in. In her distressed state, Mom decided the easiest way to handle it was to have my brother and his friends take it apart and carry it out piece by piece.

No one intended any harm. Everyone was trying to adjust to the seismic changes in our lives. Witnessing the destruction of my piano left me devastated. Before I could process that loss, more news came.

Mom gathered us together to tell us Dad wouldn't recover enough to work again. His last operation would be his final one. For over twenty-five years, he'd loved working at the Cadillac dealership on Broadway. Now, he could no longer provide for us. They had decided to sell our house and move to Las Vegas.

The news was overwhelming. My siblings and I didn't want to leave New York, our home, our friends, or Sacred Heart. That house held everything we'd ever known. The thought of leaving filled us with dread and sadness. Our brother Billy was in his early twenties at the time and still living at home. He decided to stay in New York.

Soon, the house was filled with cardboard boxes. We packed up everything except the furniture and what we'd take on the plane. When two massive moving vans arrived, we watched as movers carried out our belongings. My heartbreak deepened as we drove to Kennedy Airport to fly to Las Vegas, leaving behind New York, our home, our brother, and the life we had loved.

Strangers in a Strange Land

I was 14 when we arrived in Las Vegas. It looked like we had flown to another planet—a bizarre, otherworldly place I could never have imagined.

The air hit me like an oven as we stepped off the plane. Las Vegas is in the Mojave Desert, and its airport was unlike anything I'd ever seen. The sounds of clinking coins and flashing lights greeted us as we walked through the terminal. Slot machines were everywhere, their buzzers competing with the crowd noise. People sat in front of them with paper cups filled with coins and drinks in hand, looking like they'd set up camp. I hoped I would wake up and find it was all a strange dream. If it wasn't…could we please just go back to the life we left behind?

Uncle Eddie's townhouse was on Paradise Road, not far from the airport and just a block from the Las Vegas Strip. It was in an adults-only complex. My older sister moved into university housing for the University of Nevada, Las Vegas, and never lived with us again. Because my brother, Billy, stayed behind in New York, our family, once five strong, had dwindled to just three—Mom, Dad, and me—living with Uncle Eddie in his townhouse.

Nothing about Las Vegas felt like home. The flat terrain, stucco houses, pebble landscaping, and sparse desert plants were so stark compared to the leafy green neighborhoods we left behind. The desert stretched endlessly, with purple mountains shimmering in the distance. Driving down the strip on our first day in our uncle's Cadillac, we passed massive casinos adorned with tens of thousands of neon lights. Each marquee showcased the stars performing there. Uncle Eddie wanted to show us Caesars Palace, where he worked as the stage manager.

Caesars was the crown jewel of the strip, exuding elegance with its towering white marble pillars and statues of Greek gods. It had a long circular driveway lined with huge water fountains that shot high into the air and sparkled with lights. As we slowly drove around the driveway, I couldn't help but feel overwhelmed. Across the street stood the Flamingo Hotel. When we got to the end of the driveway, we turned left back out onto the strip. We continued past the Stardust, the Sands, the Tropicana, the Silver Slipper, and many souvenir shops, ending our tour at the Golden Nugget on Fremont Street. The area was so brightly lit that you couldn't tell whether it was day or night.

Back at Eddie's townhouse, I felt lost. I went swimming in the pool in the middle of the complex during the day, and at night went along with Uncle Eddie to work as much as I could. The complex was eerily quiet during the day, as most adults worked at night and slept during the day. But going backstage with Uncle Eddie at Caesars was a thrill.

He had an office in the backstage area. I'd go with him, and then he'd take me down to the stage area behind the massive velvet curtains, where I'd sit and watch shows from a pair of chairs that he'd have set up. My sister never came. I loved the energy of the theater. Sometimes I'd get to meet or see the legendary entertainers such as Tony Bennett, Frank Sinatra, The Jackson Five, Ike and Tina Turner, and many more, as they walked around backstage Meeting Liberace was especially thrilling for me. At the end of his dazzling performances, the lights would dim, leaving only the glow of candelabras around his piano and the tiny lights sewn into his suit jacket. He was larger than life, charming the audience with his brilliance and charisma. Uncle Eddie always said, "The bigger the star, the nicer they are."

Our bond deepened as he shared the world of show business with me. I loved going to work with him and being backstage.

Pictured below: me with Liberace at age 14 picture courtesy of Lynch Family Photos and Eddie backstage with showgirls, picture courtesy of Minsky's Burlesque Records, 1922-1978. MS-00290. Special Collections and Archives, University Libraries, University of Nevada, Las Vegas. Las Vegas, Nevada.

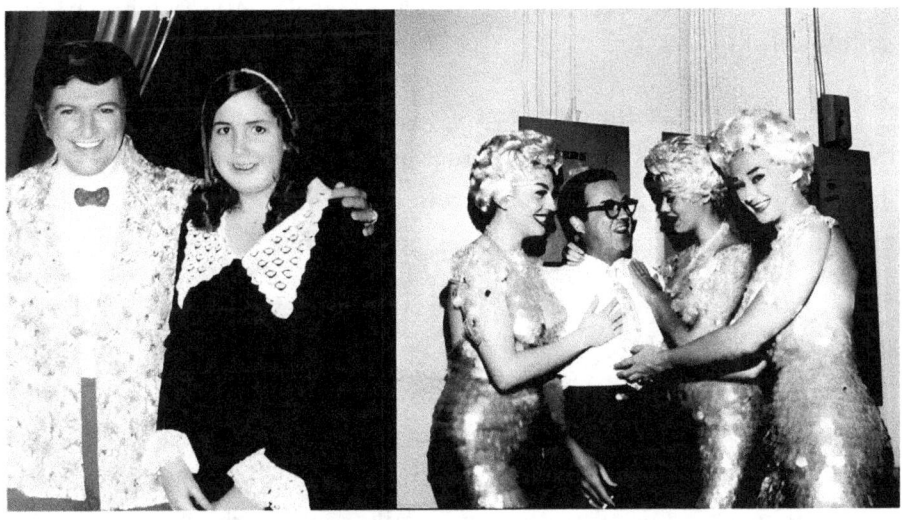

A few weeks after arriving, we moved from Eddie's two-story townhouse to a smaller one-story townhouse across the lawn. I missed New York deeply and counted the days until school started, hoping for a semblance of normalcy. In the meantime, the world Eddie introduced me to became a refuge— a place where I felt inspired and alive amidst the upheaval of our lives.

Eddie must have been an exceptionally talented young person. He might have gotten into performing as a way to get out of running bootleg for his mom. At some point, he was discovered by Al Jolson, a Lithuanian-born American singer, actor, and vaudevillian. He was one of the United States' most famous and highest-paid stars of the 1920s, self-billed as "The World's Greatest Entertainer." He worked briefly with George Gershwin before taking over managing Eddie's career. Vaudeville variety acts and the world of burlesque overlapped during that time and was the most popular form of live entertainment. There are newspaper articles about Eddie and his musical journey archived in the Minsky's Burlesque Records, 1922-1978. MS-00290. Special Collections and Archives, University Libraries, University of Nevada, Las Vegas. Las Vegas, Nevada.

Eddie met and became a friends with Harold Minsky while he was working in New York.

Harold became an owner of a place called the Gaiety Theater at the age of 19. It was located at Broadway and 46th Street and opened in 1934. It featured strip-tease dancers, burlesque acts, and baggy-pants comedians. Harold called the burlesque shows that he produced "follies."

It was during prohibition, and Harold's shows were considered to be too "raunchy." In 1943, Mayor La Guardia ordered all burlesque theaters closed in New York. Harold had to shut down his show and head out of town. Harold moved his shows to such places as Chicago, Illinois; Hollywood, California; Miami, Florida; Newark, New Jersey; and Cincinnati, Ohio, introducing "family style" burlesque and "ladies' day" to entice women to attend.

After introducing burlesque to Las Vegas, Nevada, in 1957 at the Dunes Hotel and Casino, Minsky produced shows at the Thunderbird Hotel, the Aladdin Hotel and Casino, the Silver Slipper Hotel and Casino, the Fremont Hotel and Casino, and the Frontier Hotel. A book based on the stage productions, entitled The Night They Raided Minsky's, was published in 1960 and was followed by a motion picture of the same name in 1967.

Eddie left New York in the mid 1960's and went out to Las Vegas where he had a business relationship with Harold. With Harold's help, Eddie made the change from working on the performing side of show business to working on the business side of show business, handling contracts for entertainers and show girls. He worked as a producer and a director, and by the time we moved out to Vegas, he had become the stage manager of Caesars Palace's Circus Maximus, where he worked for twenty years until he passed away in 1986.

During the years that Eddie was in Vegas and our family was still in New York, he'd fly back to New York and buy a new Cadillac for either himself or a show business friend and then drive it back to Vegas. Eddie and his ties to show business kept our family going for a long time.

Picture of Eddie backstage, courtesy of Minsky's Burlesque Records, 1922-1978. MS-00290. Special Collections and Archives, University Libraries, University of Nevada, Las Vegas. Las Vegas, Nevada.

Two Misfits Starting a New
School in Eighth Grade

School was still three months away from starting after we moved to Vegas, so I got my first job working at Orange Julius in the Boulevard Mall, the largest mall in Las Vegas. I was still 14. I had a uniform and a paper hat. Orange Julius was located on Maryland Parkway, a very busy street that runs parallel to the strip. I was waiting for my mom to pick me up one day after work when I saw Diana Ross drive by in a snappy red sports car. I had first seen her on the Ed Sullivan Show in New York when I was in second grade. I'll never forget those performances and the impact that they had on me. Every time I saw her perform, I was completely mesmerized. I never got to meet her or to hear her perform live ... just to see her whizz by me that day with her hair flying in the breeze with a big smile on her beautiful face.

When school finally started, I started eighth grade at a Catholic school. It's never easy to be the new kid, especially in eighth grade. That's supposed to be your final year that you go through with the kids that you've known since first grade. When you're a new kid in eighth grade, nobody wants to be your friend. Everybody already has their friends.

There was only one other girl who was also starting in the eighth grade, BonnieBelle.

Bonnie and I sat together to eat lunch because nobody wanted to be her friend either. Bonnie was everything that I wasn't—Vegas-born, rebellious, and uninterested in school. She HATED school, and she HATED to have to take piano lessons, which I found beyond annoying. She was boy-crazy, smoked cigarettes, experimented with drugs, and even found shoplifting entertaining. Despite coming from a well-off family who lived in a big, beautiful new house—her father was a TWA Pilot with a den adorned with a life-sized poster of John Wayne—she craved danger and excitement. She made really bad choices and did really stupid things.

BonnieBelle was blonde, model-pretty, and very mature-looking for her age. She always dressed in the best and most stylish clothes. She wore makeup and looked more like she was about seventeen. I looked like what I was...a 14-year-old who still had braces, headgear, and a clear adolescent awkwardness. While she exuded confidence, I struggled to adjust to life in Vegas, longing for my piano and the familiarity of New York.

When we lived in New York, I was an honor roll student, and I loved my old school. I'd fallen in love with learning. I loved my piano, my lessons, and going to Sacred Heart. We had a really great life. Everything in Las Vegas was the opposite, including BonnieBelle.

I'd go over to her house and have to wait for her to get through with her twenty-minute piano practice after listening to her complain, "Oh, I HATE piano lessons!" so that we could go to the mall.

We were complete opposites, but at least I had somebody to eat lunch with. She liked to have me tag along with her on her little escapades, and sometimes I did, but I was totally uncomfortable. I didn't know anything about drugs, didn't care about having a boyfriend, and I sure didn't want to smoke cigarettes, knowing what they'd done to my dad's health. Bonnie liked all of it and wanted me to participate, but I didn't like any of the things that she liked to do.

One day, she told me that she'd gotten "busted" for shoplifting. I'm not sure of what actually happened. "My car got pulled over by the police, and they tore it apart!" After that, I stopped eating lunch with her and hanging out with her. It became a really lonely time. I didn't have my piano, and now I really didn't have any friends, but Bonnie wasn't much of a friend anyway, just somebody to eat lunch with.

Desperately wanting to belong, I decided to run for class president. Nights were spent practicing saying words in my bedroom, trying to soften my thick New York accent. Our last name was Lynch. My campaign slogan was, "It's a Cinch with Lynch." It felt clever to me, but the only vote I received was my own. I just didn't fit in.

I kept trying to make friends and kept hoping that things would get better, but they didn't. I kept working at Orange Julius. At least it was something to do, and I started saving my money.

Eighth grade ended without any fanfare. There wasn't any graduation ceremony. That was disappointing. My next big hope was that high school would be better. It wasn't. The same kids who were in eighth grade were now in high school. I needed something to change, so I got myself a different job. I started working at Taco Bell, a few blocks closer to home than Orange Julius.

My boss's was named Connie. She was at least ten years older than me. She was shorter than me, had snow-white hair, and a super short haircut. She had red, blotchy skin, a low, growly voice, and buck teeth. She also had a "lazy eye." I'd look at her and could never could tell which one of her eyes was the one looking at me. I didn't know what to make of her. I was fourteen, listening to my new boss tell me what to do. We wore matching uniforms with paper hats.

One day, she asked me,"Would you like to come over to one of my friend's houses after work?" I don't know why, but I said, "OK." She took me over to an apartment that had a bunch of Black guys sitting around with curlers in their hair. I didn't know it, but they were pimps. I didn't even know what a "pimp" was. Connie was somehow working with them in the sex industry. She brought me over because she thought that they might like me. I didn't know anything about prostitution or people working in the sex industry. As soon Connie took me into the apartment, and I saw them, I felt completely uncomfortable. I told her that wanted to go home. Instead of taking me herself, she had one of the guys who were there drive me home.

I was now fifteen and still living in the apartment complex with my parents. When the guy pulled into the parking lot behind our apartment, he stopped to let me out and said, "You better get out while you still can." I got out of that car as fast as I could and ran into our apartment. It was a chilling experience. I didn't really have anyone to talk to about it. My parents were so busy just getting by and taking care of themselves that I pretty much had to look out for myself. I realized that I was going to have to be a lot more careful. I learned to never trust anybody that I didn't know, like Connie. I trusted her because she was my boss. I could see that she looked really weird and "off," but I was so young that I didn't know about the dangers.

I was an adolescent, becoming a young woman in a very dangerous and bizarre city. I kept working, going to school and kept saving my money. I stayed away from Connie. Not too long after that incident, she quit coming to work. We never saw her again. She was replaced by a guy named Tom. He was my new boss. He was nice, and he was professional. It was a relief to not have Connie there anymore. She was involved in a very dangerous business. It seemed to suit her somehow. She seemed to like what she was doing, or maybe she had just accepted it. I felt sorry for her and wondered what ever happened to her. She just disappeared one day, and no one seemed to notice.

My mom had PROMISED me before we left New York that after we moved to Vegas that, we would buy a new house and that we'd have a new home. She took me to look at houses that were for sale all the time. I'd fall in love with them and imagine us living there. They always had a pool. What a great way to make friends! Our parents had enough money from the sale of our house in Yonkers to buy a house, but our dad never wanted the responsibility of being a home owner again. I would tell her, "Mom.. it's perfect! Can we buy it?" I didn't know that in the 1970's a woman couldn't buy or even own her own property, at least not in Nevada. My mom couldn't talk my dad into buying a house, so we never owned another home.

Our father went on to live for another ten years after we moved to Vegas, but he was never the same. He found it very hard to communicate with people. His voice was very weak when he spoke. It was very strained and just barely above a whisper. He was never able to work again. He felt defeated, and he became depressed. His gregarious style was gone. He lived like a ghost among us. He tried to maintain the image of a man with a job, taking care of his family, but mostly, he drove around in an old pink Buick and bet on the horses, hoping that somehow his ship might still come in.

Our parents finally moved out of the townhouse and went on to rent two different houses, but I wasn't happy. A rental house didn't feel like a HOME. I wanted us to have our OWN home again. I kept working, going to school, and saving my money.

By the time that I was 17, I had saved enough to buy myself my first car. It was my dream car. A metallic blue 1967 Chevy Camaro convertible. I bought it for $600.00. I used my savings and my mom to help me get a car loan for $200.00 to pay for the rest of it. After I paid it off, I began making plans to move out of my parents second rental house. We had been living in Las Vegas for 3 years and had lived in a townhouse and 2 rental houses. My mom had been driving me around the whole time, looking at houses to buy. I knew after 3 years of looking at houses and being disappointed so many times that it wasn't going to happen, as much as she and I wanted to believe that it would. The rental houses never felt like a home, and we never felt like a family again after we moved to Vegas. My older brother and sister were not around. My sister lived in UNLV housing and my brother stayed in New York. I knew that I was going to have to find my own way.

I became filled with a relentless drive to succeed. I kept the picture of my piano teacher playing his concert in my imagination...imagining that it was me in the picture. I'd lost sight of it for a while after I lost my piano and we moved to Vegas. Being at Bonnie's house and listening to her complain about her having to do her practice for her piano lessons helped to bring the picture back into focus and brought an even stronger drive and determination to succeed. I knew who I was and what I wanted to do. I was going to figure it out. I was going to succeed, no matter what. I wanted to have the security of having a home and a family again. I wanted a piano and to take lessons again. I decided that to have those things, I was going to have to set out on my own and someday, somehow, get them for myself.

I was still 17 when I finished paying my car off. I found an apartment in the same apartment complex that my older sister lived in. I quit Bishop Gorman High School and enrolled in Las Vegas Night School. I got myself a job working at a catering company called Chefs Orchid. It was near the end of the strip, next to McCarran Airport, and about a mile from my new apartment.

My job was assembly line work. It was hard, boring work. We had to lift big plastic green flats of dirty silverware and put them into an industrial dishwasher. Then we had to dry them with towels and, put sets of a knife, fork, and a spoon into a plastic bag, and then seal each set with a different machine. Then, we'd put the sets into boxes that were very heavy. We'd have to have somebody lift them onto a wire rack shelving unit where somebody else would come and get them. Eventually, they'd be put together with meals made by the catering company and be taken with the food to planes to be served to the passengers. We did this over and over for 8 hours a day. I worked with a bunch of old ladies who wore hair nets. I was the only young person. I worked from 7:00 a.m. until 3:00 p.m. That got me back to my apartment just in time to change clothes and drive myself to night school.

I listened to music every chance I got. I listened to the radio in my Camaro and had an eight-track player in my apartment. I loved music so much. I knew that somehow, someday, music would be my life. I kept believing that if I stayed true to myself and that if I just kept going and kept that picture of my piano teacher in my mind that someday, my heart's desire to become a professional pianist, to have a home, and to a have a family of my own would all come true. I was unstoppable. I stayed absolutely steadfast in my dreams. That was going to be my life. Someday. Somehow.

Being 17, I lived on a diet of M&M's and coffee during the week and made French toast for myself in my new apartment on the weekends. French toast was the only thing that I knew how to make.

After a long week of working with the old ladies at Chef's Orchid and going to night school, having a day off and enjoying my French toast was something that I really looked forward to and relished. I smothered my stack of French toast with butter and syrup and savored every bite. I was completely fueled by coffee and sugar. I wanted to go swimming on the weekends at the pool at the apartment complex where I lived, but I was too uncomfortable to go there by myself. I felt unprotected and vulnerable being by myself. I was not comfortable being alone in the world at 17. I kept my focus on working, going to school, and saving my money.

After I got settled into my apartment, my new job at the catering company, and night school, I started visiting my older sister at her apartment on the weekends for something to do. Her apartment was not far from mine. She was 7 years older and living an entirely different experience than me. She had already finished a few years at Hunter College and was working on finishing her bachelor's degree at UNLV. I was working on finishing high school.

I watched my older sister to see what she was doing. I didn't have anyone else to look up to or any adults looking out for me to give me guidance. I thought that my older sister looked like she knew what she was doing. She was in college. She had a steady boyfriend who had moved in with her. He was also in college. She and her boyfriend were both 24, and I was still 17. Her boyfriend had a best friend named Steve, who was a little older. He was 26. I'd run into him sometimes when I'd go to visit my sister. I saw that he drove a '68 yellow Camaro, and that caught my attention. We had something in common. After seeing him several more times at her apartment, we began to go on dates. He became my first boyfriend and the only boyfriend I'd ever had. I'd been way too busy working to get my apartment, going to night school, and working all day to think about having a boyfriend. My relationship with him developed, and within 2 years, he asked me to marry him. I said, "Yes."

I called my brother in New York to tell him the news. He said, "Don't do it! Don't get married! You're too young to get married!" He was so far away, and I wanted to move forward in life. He was right, but I didn't listen.

I was 19. I didn't know that you needed a marriage license to get married. Nobody had ever mentioned it. We had a wedding ceremony in the woods about sixty miles north of Vegas in a place called Mount Charleston. Steve had a house there. My mom had a best friend named Diane who had been a professional singer and had had her own TV show at one time. She had a house with a pool and lived close to where my parents were living in Vegas in their second rental house.

My mom's friend had become some kind of a minister, and she told my mom that she'd be happy to marry us. I bought a beautiful white wedding dress with a veil, invited some friends, and planned a ceremony to take place outside in the woods at Mount Charleston. When the day came, I put on my wedding dress. My dad was there to walk me down a little path to where my mother's friend, Diane, performed our service. Steve and I had written out our own vows that we said to each other. After that, Diane said some words and then sang "You Fill Up My Senses" by John Denver. It was a nice service, and I believed that we were married. I changed my last name to his just by starting to use it.

I moved into Steve's house in Mt. Charleston. It was a nice house in the mountains. I was there all day with 2 dogs while Steve worked Mondays through Fridays in Vegas as a buyer for a school district. It took him an hour to drive each way, and then he spent 8 hours a day at work, so he was gone a lot.

He had a turn table in his living room and a very limited record collection. I soon became bored and restless. I wanted to be married because I thought that being married would help me to create a stable family life, to get a home and a piano and get back to taking lessons. I never told Steve about my burning ambition to become a professional pianist. Music wasn't something that we had in common. I knew that Steve wanted us to be happy, so I thought that in time, everything would work out.

I had seen so many of the great performers on the Ed Sullivan show when I was young and then later had the experience of meeting and hearing so many of the greatest musicians of all time backstage at Caesar's Palace. I knew there was a whole world of music out there and that, somehow I had to find a way to find my place in it.

I didn't have a piano at our house in Mt. Charleston. Steve had no idea of what I wanted to do with my life or of how determined I was to find a way to do it. We had just never talked about it. He was 9 years older than me and very content with his life. I was 19, restless and bored. I had to figure out how to explain to him that we were going to have to change some things to build a happy life together.

My boredom grew from not having a piano and being alone so much that I started taking painting lessons from a woman who lived in Vegas just for something to do. She showed me photos of some property that she owned in Washington state. It looked so beautiful. After seeing the photos that my art teacher showed me, I decided that I wanted to go to the Pacific Northwest. I thought that it would be a beautiful place to go and that maybe it would be a place where, eventually, we could have a home, I could get a piano, take piano lessons again, and Steve could go to college. I thought that maybe we could build a happy life there together.

I talked Steve into quitting his job and moving there. He found something that he was interested in enough to enroll in college in a town called Ashland in southern Oregon while I carried the quiet, unwavering dream of finding my way back to music.

I never told him or anyone about what had happened to my piano in New York. Though I never shared my aspirations with him, the image of my piano teacher remained vivid in my mind. It was my compass, guiding me through uncertainty as I worked tirelessly to build the life I dreamed of.

I thought that getting married would give me the stability that I needed to figure things out and build a happy life together. Steve was actually very content with his life in Mount Charleston. He only moved to Oregon to make me happy and because, somehow, I'd talked him into it. I was still so young. I was still just a kid, trying to live a grown-up life.

Leaving Las Vegas

We packed up and moved to Ashland, Oregon. It was beautiful. It looked just like the pictures that I'd seen with the big green evergreen trees and lush nature all around. Ashland was a tiny little town - a postcard town with really nothing for me to do there either. The main attraction was a bar downtown, but I wasn't even old enough to walk through the door. Steve started his classes at the college there, but I was restless and bore again, without a piano or much else to do.

Twenty miles north, there was a slightly bigger town called Medford. I went to the unemployment office there to see if they could help me find a job. A woman there gave me an aptitude test.

"You scored exceptionally high in mechanical drawing," she said. Mechanical drawing? I wasn't sure of what that was. "Do you want to try a job in drafting?" she asked, holding out a paper with an address on it.

It was a great job - a drafting position that required a two-year certificate. I had no qualifications beyond my test results, but they needed someone. I drove out and met the man who was hiring, and just like that, I got the job.

I loved it. I had my own drafting table, and I learned how to design business forms.

It wasn't music, but it was creative, and it made me feel like I was moving forward in life. The pay wasn't bad either. I'd discovered something important about myself: working and saving my money gave me options, and options meant freedom. I was moving forward in life and happy that we'd moved out of Las Vegas.

At home, though, things were unraveling. Steve had bought himself a guitar. He'd sit on the couch strumming it—out of tune—and sing in a voice that could peel paint off the walls. I think he might have been tone-deaf. I'd escape to the bedroom, burying my head in a pillow to drown out the noise.

Day after day, the guitar playing continued. It was hideous, and I began to realize that I'd made a big mistake. I couldn't see a future with him. There wasn't any harmony—not in his music, not in our lives.

While Steve kept strumming and singing, I started to make a plan. I worked hard, saved every penny, and when I finally had enough, I gave my notice at the drafting job. One day, while Steve was out, I sat down at the kitchen table and wrote him a letter. "Dear Steve, I'm sorry, but I think it's best for both of us if I move on with my life. I hope you understand."... or something like that.

I signed it, folded it neatly, and left it on the table. I packed my things, got in my car, and left. I didn't know what lay ahead, but I knew I couldn't stay.

My sister had moved to Eugene, Oregon, about two hours north of Ashland. She was going to the university there. I set out for Eugene to get a new start and to figure out how to move forward with my life, without Steve.

I stopped in at a courthouse along the way to find out how to get a divorce. It was there that I learned that I'd never been married in the first place because we never had a marriage license. A clerk at the courthouse checked the records, and after checking, he said, "There's no record of you having a marriage license, so you're not married."

I blinked. Just like that, it was over. There wasn't anything that I needed to do except to get into my car and continue on my way to visit my sister in Eugene. I went back to using my maiden name.

After I got to Eugene, I stayed with my sister and her husband for a few days. It was a little awkward. Her husband was the same boyfriend that she'd had in Las Vegas and was still Steve's best friend, although no one brought it up. My sister suggested that I check out a co-op in town to look for a place to live. I found a bulletin board there that had an ad posted by some people who were looking for a roommate. I called the number and went over.

I met Barney and Carl, who were both from Boston. Barney was going to the university in Eugene, and Carl had graduated from a prep school. Carl loved to draw tiny cartoons, was writing a science fiction book, and he loved to cook. He made the best soups and the best coffee I'd ever had.

The other roommate was a girl named Sherri. She looked about sixteen, with thin blonde hair and foggy wire-rimmed glasses. She didn't wear makeup or a bra, which made it easy to see that she was very top-heavy. Sherri laughed at absolutely everything—a strange, airy laugh that made you wonder if she understood the conversation at all. She was a nutty, free-wheeling spirit who seemed completely untethered from reality.

Sherri went to a party one night, and not too long after that, she told us that she was pregnant and that she had no idea of who the father was. Fortunately, not too long after that, her parents came and got her. They came just in time. She had just started to try and learn how to play the violin. The sounds that came from her room were horrific. It was such a relief for us when her parents came and took pregnant Sherri and her violin home with them. She really needed her family. We never saw her again.

Life in Eugene was different. I wasn't sure where I was heading yet, but for the first time in a while, I felt like I was on my own path. I was free to dream again, and I was determined to figure out what came next.

Saving the Dog and my Burning Van

I got myself a job as a waitress in Eugene, working a split shift at a Mexican restaurant about six miles away from our house. My car had broken down, so I had no choice but to ride the bus twice a day while I saved up my tip money. Every night, I'd come home exhausted, dropping crumpled dollar bills and loose change into a jar on my dresser. I watched that jar fill slowly, hopeful that I'd soon have enough to buy a car.

After I finally saved up $600, I called my sister to see if she knew anybody who had a car that I could buy. She said that she did. I bought a Ford van from some guy that she knew. It had a giant crack in the windshield. The guy told me, "It's really dependable. You'll love it."

I trusted my sister and relied on her judgment more than the van itself, so I handed over the cash. I'd never driven a van before. It steered like steering a boat. I hung a crystal ball from the rear view mirror, hoping its shine would help me forget about the glaring crack in the windshield. I was always looking on the bright side of things.

Buying the van did make life a lot easier. I didn't have to rely on buses anymore, but now I was driving one. One night after my late shift at the Mexican restaurant, I climbed into the van, exhausted. The wind howled, rain hammered against the roof, and the darkness felt heavy. I turned the key. Nothing.

I tried again. The engine didn't even cough—it just sat there, dead. I turned to look behind me and was shocked. I saw flames. The battery, which sat directly behind the driver's seat, was on fire. My heart jumped into my throat. I flung the door open and leaped out into the storm, stumbling across the parking lot as fast as I could. Rain soaked through my clothes, mixing with the sweat of panic. I kept running, thinking that the van might explode behind me. When I finally stopped to look back, I saw it: my van, with a faint glow flickering through the rain. It hadn't exploded. It was just sitting there, broken and with a flaming battery, a sad testament to my $600 investment.

It was a dark, cold, windy, rainy, and miserable night. I didn't have anybody to call. We didn't have cell phones then, and I didn't have anybody to call anyway. All I could do was to start walking home along the highway. The wind shoved against me as I kept moving, step by step, along the empty highway. I kept walking for miles until I reached an overpass. Finally, I could see our house in the distance, a faint light cutting through the rain.

Then I heard it—a sound that sliced through the storm. An animal crying out in pain. The sound came from beneath the overpass. I couldn't leave it. I slid down the muddy hill, my shoes slipping and my clothes growing heavier with every step.

At the bottom, I found him. A medium-sized dog curled up and trembling in pain. He'd been hit by a car and somehow ended up there, alone. His soft cries were muffled by the rain, and when I bent to pick him up, he snapped at the air near my face—close enough to make me flinch.

"It's okay, buddy," I whispered, my voice shaking. "It's gonna be okay."

He was hurt and scared. He was having a worse night than I was. I lifted him up and held him. His body was warm, his cries sharp as I carried him back up the muddy slope. Rain ran down my face like tears, but I didn't stop. One step at a time, I made it to the road. Headlights appeared in the distance. A city bus. I flagged it down, holding the injured dog tightly in my arms. The bus screeched to a stop. The driver opened the door, his eyes widening when he saw me—soaked, shivering, and cradling the dog.

"Please," I begged. "He's hurt. I don't have far to go." The driver shook his head. "No animals."

"But he's hurt," I pleaded. The driver repeated, "No, you can't bring him on the bus."

My heart sank. I stepped back and waved the bus on, watching as its taillights disappeared into the night. With no other choice, I kept walking. My arms ached from carrying the dog, but I wasn't going to leave him. Step by step, we made it home. I carried him the half mile further to our house through the storm.

Carl answered the door as soon as I got there. He'd seen me coming. He took one look at me—a dripping, muddy mess holding a trembling dog—and sprang into action.

"Come inside!" he said, pulling the door open wide.

Carl wrapped the dog in blankets and brought me towels and dry clothes. The house was warm, and Carl's kindness softened the sharp edges of the night. We found a tag on the dog's collar and called his owner. While we waited, Carl made hot chocolate for us. The dog wanted to go under a table, so we let him go, with his blanket falling off around him. His eyes looked scared, and although he was hurt, he'd stopped crying as he looked out at us from under the table.

"Boy, it looks like you've had quite a night," Carl teased, handing me a steaming mug. "You could say that," I said, managing a smile. The owner finally arrived. He wasn't excited or relieved to see his dog—he seemed irritated, as if this was an inconvenience. He didn't even thank me. He took the dog, muttered something, and left. What a night. At least the little dog was saved and I had made it home. I took a shower and went to bed, exhausted.

The next day was Sunday. It was my only day off. After I got up, Carl made me some of his famous coffee and one of his fantastic soups. He always fed me, no matter how rushed I was. I was very thin from working so hard, working those double shifts. "You've got to eat something," he'd say, like a mother hen. He was very comforting and had become a good friend. We both liked to laugh and to share jokes.

When I left my van the night before, I took the keys with me. I didn't take time to lock it.

I took the city bus back to the parking lot, expecting to find a burnt-out shell of my van. But when I got there, my van looked... fine. I couldn't believe it! I looked it over, walked around it and then opened the door and climbed in. There was no evidence of a fire. There weren't even any black marks on the battery. I put the key in the ignition, turned the key, and - miraculously, it started!

I sat there for a moment, stunned. It was like the night before had never happened.

It was both a mystery and a miracle. Maybe an angel had been watching, and saving the dog had been my reward. Either way, I was so happy and relieved. I was ready to move forward again. I wanted to stop working at the Mexican restaurant and to get out of Eugene.

Right about that time, I got the news that my dad had passed away in Vegas. I went back for his funeral. My grief-stricken uncle stood in the back of the church wearing dark sunglasses. My brother was sick and didn't come out from New York. I held my mom's arm as we walked down the aisle to a pew near his casket. I don't remember much else from that day.

When I returned to Oregon, I brought back a pair of jumper cables that had been my dad's. I've kept them in the trunk of every car that I've owned since, a small piece of him that has stayed with me wherever I go. Those jumper cables have come in handy more times than I can count, but more than that, they've been a comfort—a reminder that he's still with me, riding along.

Even in the worst moments, I always kept going and found a way to move forward.

The Oregon Coast and My Artistic Soul

After I returned from my father's funeral, I put my jumper cables into my van and decided to take a drive over over to the Oregon Coast, about an hour west of Eugene. The drive took me through the Cascade Mountain Range, a winding ribbon of road surrounded by towering Douglas firs. The air smelled rich and clean, like rain and pine. Moss hung from tree branches, thick and green, with giant ferns that sprawled across the forest floor like nature's carpet. Everything felt alive, ancient, and endless. It was as though I had stumbled into a natural cathedral, a quiet and awe-inspiring, majestical botanical garden.

After I reached the crest of a bend, I gasped. The road opened up, and there it was—the Oregon Coast. It spread out before me, wild and magnificent, waves crashing against jagged rocks like a symphony only nature could conduct. The sky was gray and moody, the kind of sky that promised storms and secrets. I pulled over to take it all in. I'd never seen anything so beautiful—so raw, so powerful, and untamed. It was breathtakingly spectacular, like nothing I'd ever seen before.

The road led me to Highway 101, the iconic coastal route that stretches endlessly in both directions. I turned left, heading south, passing through a tiny postage stamp size of a town called "Yachats." The waves were visible from the highway, colossal and hypnotic. I felt as if I'd discovered something magical like the coast had been waiting for me all along.

It was the most stunningly beautiful and wild place that I'd ever seen. It had an energy and a magic quality to it that made me so happy to be there. It was a real adventure. I fell in love with it and decided right then that I was going to move there. I continued driving South and drove up a long, steep hill that wound higher and higher until I reached a lookout point marked "Cape Foulweather." The name made me smile— it seemed fitting. The wind had howled with such force that the trees lining the cape had half their branches stripped bare, all on one side. It was like they'd been combed by nature itself. I parked for a few minutes and watched the waves explode against the rocks below. It was brutal and beautiful all at once, the kind of place that made you feel small in the best possible way. I started the van again and started driving, this time heading down the other side. I turned in at the next turn-off spot, about a half mile past the lookout point. I felt that I'd had enough adventure for my first day.

I turned around and headed back north again towards the tiny little town of Yachats. I drove through it and continued about a mile further north. I spotted a driveway leading to a place called "The Adobe Resort." It sat close to the ocean, surrounded by beautifully manicured lawns and giant exotic plants and flowers. I turned down the driveway and parked in the parking lot.

I climbed out of my van and walked through the double doors. I didn't see any people inside. I saw a gift shop off to the right. I went inside and looked around in it, thinking there might be somebody in there, but there wasn't anybody in there either. I went back out to the hallway and saw two big glass doors at the end of the hallway.

I went up to the doors. They were locked. I pressed my hands against the glass, peering inside. Beyond the doors was a formal dining room, elegant and pristine. The tables were covered in starched white tablecloths, each set with fresh flowers and silverware. Enormous windows framed the ocean like a moving painting. The tables were arranged so that each one had an ocean view. As I stood there looking, I noticed a couple coming up the hallway behind me.

They said hello and introduced themselves. "Hello, I'm Jack, and this is my wife, Laura." Laura was holding a little white poodle in her arms. Jack asked, "Are you here to apply for the waitress position?"

He had a relaxed friendly face, and Laura looked like somebody had stolen her out of a wax museum. She was super skinny with jet-black hair pulled up tight in a French twist. She had on very heavy makeup with thick black eyelashes and bright red lipstick. Nothing on her face seemed to move. She had a pleasant expression, but her face looked frozen, and I'm not sure she blinked. She was impeccably dressed in a fitted tweed wool skirt with a matching jacket and a neck scarf. Her French twist was done to perfection. Her face was very thin and chiseled, a bit like a prehistoric bird. She had an elegance about her and a quality of being very self-controlled and formal. Definitely, no-nonsense.

I answered, "Oh, yes, I'm here to apply." not knowing anything about it.

Laura gave me a look that felt like an appraisal, then nodded. "Follow me."

She led me through the beautiful dining room and then showed me into the kitchen, explaining and showing me how the waitresses placed their orders. Her tone was brisk and formal, as though she were interviewing someone far more qualified than I was. I followed her back out to the dining room, and we sat down at one of the tables. She said, "You can start tomorrow. Please be here at 4:00 p.m. I'll have a senior waitress here to go over everything with you before the restaurant opens at 5:00 p.m."

I blinked, caught off guard. "Oh! Thank you. I'll be here."

As I walked back down the hallway, I passed the gift shop and went outside to my van, my heart raced. I had just landed a job at this stunning place without even trying. I hoped they wouldn't see my old Ford van sitting in the lot. It didn't look like something that Laura would like to see parked at the Adobe.

I went into a little town just a few miles north and found a used clothing store. I bought a white blouse and a black skirt and found a place to buy some nylons. Fortunately, I had my black leather "Mary Jane" waitressing shoes in my van. I had my outfit. I was all set. I had even found a laundromat with an iron so I could press my blouse and my skirt. I was determined to show up looking like I belonged at The Adobe.

That night, I slept in my van. I parked in a parking lot for tourists to park in while they explored the trails that led to the beach off the highway. I listened to the soothing sounds of the waves as I went to sleep. They were close by, just beyond the trails and giant pieces of driftwood that were scattered all over the beach.

When I woke up the next morning, I opened the van door and saw the beauty that surrounded me. I found a bathroom in the corner of the parking lot. There wasn't anyone else in the parking lot or in the bathroom. I was able to wash my face and carefully apply my make-up. I put on my outfit that I had carefully hung up in my van and carefully tied my hair up with a hair tie. When it was time to go to the Adobe, I was as prepared as I could be. I was excited and ready to begin my new adventure!

I arrived at the Adobe and parked in a place that was out of view of the main doors. It was a little before 4:00 p.m. I took a deep breath and went in to begin my new job.

I met Laura in the hallway just outside of the dining room with a young woman dressed in a waitress outfit like mine. Laura looked me over and then said with approval, "Let me introduce you to Sara. Sara is a senior waitress who will show you around and teach you about the wine selection." With that, Laura left. Sara said, "Hello, Maureen. Nice to meet you. I'll show you our wine selection and explain how it works." She led me over to a large wine case. She showed me how to open a bottle, to then let the people who'd ordered it sniff the cork, and then "pour just enough for someone to swirl it around in their wine glass and then take a sip to make sure they like it." She showed me how to write up orders, and she gave me a black satin waist-high apron with big pockets in the front. It had to be tied in the back into a perfect bow. All of the waitresses had to be looked over by Laura before we could go out into the dining room to go to work. She made sure that we and our outfits had a look that represented the professional and first-class standards of the Adobe. She made sure that our bows were tied and fluffed just right.

"It's about standards," she said firmly, eyeing us like a drill sergeant.

The main chef was a cheery older lady name Edie. Edie always had a smile. She was always super cheerful, and she always tried to hide how stressed out and nervous she was when Laura showed up. Laura was intimidating to all of us, but she really got to Edie. Edie wore a starched white chef's uniform and a towering chef's hat. She made the best razor clams in the world. Every night, she'd crank out hundreds of orders. Her most requested orders were for her own recipe for lobster thermidor, a beautiful bubbly hot casserole, and her filet mignon steaks that she cooked to perfection. The razor clams were only available on the lunch menu. They were heavenly. Laura included a meal for her waitresses. We got to eat in the dining room and watch the waves when the restaurant was closed. I had the razor clams as often as possible. We worked hard and fast in a spectacular place. The wild Oregon coast was all around us, with its huge waves crashing up against the rocks below us. Sometimes, it changed suddenly from soothing waves rolling in over the rocks below us on moonlit nights to gigantic waves thundering in with wind and rain, smashing onto the rocks, almost up to the windows. It was all magnificent. We were in awe of nature giving us a nightly show.

I was so relieved to be out of the Mexican restaurant and not working those double shifts.

Moving to the Oregon coast and getting the job at the Adobe made my life so much better. Working at The Adobe felt like stepping into a different world. It was elegant and serene, so unlike the chaos of the Mexican restaurant I had left behind. The tips were twice what I'd been making in Eugene. Life was better—easier. I'd taken another bold step forward, and it had paid off.

I rented a little cabin in Yachats, very close to the ocean. I could hear the waves at night from my bedroom window. My commute to the Adobe was less than a mile up Hwy. 101. The combination of the magnificence of the coast and the beauty of nature there brought me a sense of peace. It was a place that helped to feed and nurture the longing in my artistic soul. I always kept the picture of my piano teacher playing his concert in my minds eye. I knew that I had a long way to go and that it might take me years to get there. I kept moving forward and kept doing things that I thought would improve my life and bring me closer to the day that it would be ME in that picture.

I started saving my money and saved up enough to sell my van and get myself a decent-looking car. One day there was a Dodge Polara parked at the bank across the street from my cabin. It was for sale. I bought it, not having any idea of how great of a car it was. My van was an embarrassment to be seen in, especially at the posh Adobe Resort. The Dodge Polara looked great. It was a car that cops used to drive. What a car! ..completely dependable.. with tons of power and built to last. It was just what I needed! I bought it, put my dad's jumper cables in the trunk, and sold my van.

My cabin was right on Hwy. 101 in a row of about four other cabins that were next to each other on a dirt road that lead to the ocean. The guy who ran the cabins lived in a bigger cabin across from our row. He was a hunched-over, barrel-shaped old guy with dark, sunken eyes who looked like Uncle Fester from the Adams Family. He would come over in person to collect the rent and he did not like my new friend, George. He'd see George's car parked across the street at the bank. He'd give it a squinty-eyed look and then look back at me. I'd smile and give him his rent money in cash, and he'd tromp off.

George was a guy about my age who also worked at the Adobe.

He never said what he actually did there. He might have been a dishwasher. We were both about 20 years old. After we met, I learned that he was a drummer from New York and that he could also play 12-string guitar and sing. I thought there might be an opportunity for me to learn about music from someone who had shown up in such an isolated and unlikely place. George was medium height, had medium-length black hair, a thin mustache, and brown beady eyes behind tinted glasses. He was a shady-looking guy, but I wanted to find out what he knew about playing music.

He came over to my cabin with his guitar to visit me and played for me. He played well, and he could sing.. in tune. After I found out that he'd had some professional experience, I overlooked everything else about him, which was like basically everything else about him. He talked me into buying his stereo for $600.00, and later on, I found out that he'd stolen it. That was George. He could play music but lacked character and was always looking out for himself.

He visited me often and told me that if I bought a guitar, he would teach me how to play it. I saved enough money and bought a 12-string guitar.

The guitar I bought was a good one. It was a Conn, exactly like his. He picked it out for me. Playing it, however, felt really awkward. It had a really wide neck, and the strings hurt my fingers. It had both nylon and steel strings. I had to build up calluses on my fingertips. George always tuned it for me, which was a blessing because tuning a 12-string was a nightmare for me. Over time, he taught me how to play and sing a lot of songs. They were popular tunes like "The House of the Rising Sun," a lot of songs by the Beatles, the Rolling Stones and the pop music at the time. He knew hundreds of songs. I was a natural at music, but the piano was my instrument. I really struggled with the 12-string, but at least I was playing an instrument and learning the chords and the songs that he taught me.

I had followed enough stepping stones to finally find someone that I could learn something about music from in the most unlikely of places, Yachats, Oregon. George felt familiar to me because he was from New York. He was from upstate. It was a part of the state that I wasn't familiar with, but he was from the state that had been my home. I wondered if it would ever be my home again.

One day, George told me that he was leaving and that he was going back to New York. He wanted to get back to working as a drummer again. He took off and called me a few weeks later after he got back. He was in a place called Saratoga Springs. It's located about 200 miles north of the City. He asked me if I wanted to move there and live with him there. My older brother had moved out of Yonkers and was living in Croton on the Hudson, about 150 miles south of Saratoga Springs, 50 miles north of the City, and 3,000 miles closer than the Oregon coast.

I gave my notice and quit my job at the Adobe. I packed up my Dodge Polara and drove from Yachats to Saratoga Springs by myself. I made it there in three nights and arrived on the fourth day. I blasted Schubert's Fantasy Impromptu on my eight-track in my car the whole way and kept that picture of my piano teacher in my minds eye. I was making another courageous move forward, once again moving to a place that I'd never been to before. I thought that there would be a lot more opportunity to pursue music in New York than at the Oregon Coast.

Following George from the Oregon Coast to Saratoga Springs, New York

When I arrived, it was mid-morning on a day in early summer. I found the house where George was staying. It was a modest one-story house sitting on a big lot adorned with fruit trees. Around it, small farmhouses dotted the landscape, surrounded by neat rows of orchards. It was serene and picturesque, yet felt like a world apart from the coastal beauty I had just left behind.

I pulled into the driveway, and George came out to greet me. He took me inside and introduced me to Stan, the owner of the house. Stan greeted me warmly. He had a laid-back demeanor and seemed genuinely kind. He showed me around his home and explained a bit about the area. George had already arranged for me to stay there, too, making me Stan's second roommate. I brought in my few belongings from the car and began settling in. I was tired from my trip and wanted to turn in for the night.

The next day, George took me to a local Italian restaurant called "Marty's," just a few miles away. The place exuded a cozy charm, and George seemed at ease there. He introduced me to Marty, the friendly owner, who immediately offered me a job as a waitress. I accepted without hesitation.

Marty's had a unique setup. The restaurant housed a gleaming grand piano, positioned so that half of it extended into the dining room and the other half into the lounge. The pianist, Gary, played soothing tunes that filled the rooms with warmth and class. I had never worked in a restaurant that served drinks, so taking bar orders alongside dinner orders was a new challenge. It was the first time that I'd be taking drink orders along with dinner orders.

After my shifts, I started going into the bar to listen to Gary play. I ordered a drink called a 7 & 7, a blend of whiskey and soda that George liked. It was really the only drink that I knew the name of, so that's what I ordered. It tasted awful. It was the first time that I'd ever gone into a bar and ordered a drink for myself. I had to order something, so that's what I ordered so that I could listen to the piano music.

Gary was an accomplished pianist who knew a lot of popular music, movie themes and classical pieces. His music created a serene atmosphere that was relaxing and enjoyable to listen to. He noticed me sitting alone at the bar and started coming over during his breaks. He was older— probably in his 40s—and always dressed in a suit. He liked to play up his role as a performer. He created a unique look for himself with his jet-black toupee, pencil-thin mustache, and a neck scarf that gave him an air of a showy style that was hard to ignore.

One evening, Gary asked to join me at my table during his break. I agreed, eager to talk about music. Our conversation was all about my curiosity about the piano and about the music that he chose to play. I asked him if he knew how to play Schubert's "Fantasy Impromptu." He was impressed with my request and played it for me later that evening, leaving me in awe. I would go in every night to listen to him after my shifts. He liked to come over and sit with me at my table. I was hoping that I could take piano lessons from him, but he said that he wasn't interested in giving piano lessons. Over time, his demeanor shifted; he started to do things like sliding his hand over the table, closer to mine and moving himself closer to me, becoming flirtatious. That made me uncomfortable. I wanted to listen to him play, but I didn't want him to sit with me anymore. I started sitting at the bar so that I'd have people on either side of me rather than sitting at a table by myself. Marty had a mirror hung up over the piano keys so people in the bar could watch his hands move as he played. I really enjoyed listening to him and watching his hands move. I'd smile and give him a little wave, but I didn't want to get to know him any better than that.

Inspired by Gary's playing, I found a local music store and bought a small electric keyboard that Stan let me set up in his living room. It was the first keyboard instrument I'd owned since losing my piano in Yonkers eight years earlier. It wasn't much, but it was a start—a milestone that signaled my return to music. I began taking lessons from a woman at the store, but they weren't as helpful as I'd hoped. She focused exclusively on sight-reading, giving me pieces that were too advanced for my skill level. I struggled to read the music that she gave me. I practiced as much as I could and realized that the music that was written was made out of the chords George had taught me on guitar. It helped me to understand how to play the songs that she gave me. The music had chord symbols. I couldn't read the notes very well, but I could understand how to play the songs using the chord symbols. I plunked out the melodies and put them together with chords and rhythm.

I was developing my own unique way of interpreting the music and making it sound good.

My time at Marty's was short-lived. I learned that the restaurant only operated during the summer, catering to vacationers from the city. As the season wound down, I began to worry about what I would do for work during the harsh upstate New York winter. The thought of snow-covered roads and limited opportunities loomed over me.

One night, as I sat on the couch after work thinking about this, Stan approached me with a serious expression. He asked if he could sit with me. I said, "sure, Stan, what's up?" He hesitated before telling me that George had been having his his ex-girlfriend over while I was at work behind my back.

Stan telling me that made my decision for me. I was not going to stay with George. I was not going to stay in Saratoga Springs and try and figure out how to survive the winter after finding out what he was up to. I called my mom.

It was perfect timing. My mom was leaving Portland a day before I could get there if I left New York the next day. That's exactly what I did. My mom was able to make arrangements with the manager for me to be able to move into her apartment as soon as I got to Portland.

Once again, I was going someplace I'd never been, trusting that something better was waiting for me. I was sorry that I would miss seeing my mom, but I was happy that I'd have her apartment waiting for me. My mom left a key for me and told me to check in with the office after I arrived to let them know that I was there.

I packed my Dodge Polara the next morning, with my dad's jumper cables in the trunk, and set out once more. Another long drive, another leap into the unknown. As I drove westward, I blasted music on my eight-track player, the music fueling my determination. The picture of my piano teacher at the Steinway burned brightly in my mind. I was chasing that vision, refusing to let anything—or anyone—stop me.

It was another bold step toward the life I was destined for. Portland awaited, offering new opportunities to follow the passion that was the heartbeat of my journey.

Leaving New York and Landing in a Jazz Club in Portland

When I left New York the next morning, I drove straight through, pulling over to rest at highway rest stops, curling up in my car for a few hours at a time before pushing forward.

I reached Portland late in the evening on the third day. The soft golden light of late August was falling over the city like a blanket. I found my mom's apartment without much trouble. It was a nice place in a clean and quiet neighborhood. I found the spot to park my car and pulled in. I summoned all of the courage that I could, landing in a strange city all alone. I had no job and no friends there, but I had a roof over my head and an unshakable belief that things would work out. I found her apartment and the key that she'd hidden for me. I felt the glow of her warmth after I entered. It was very nice, and being there calmed me. I went to bed, exhausted.

The next morning, I checked in with the office as my mom had instructed. Afterward, I stopped at a newsstand and picked up a newspaper. Sitting cross-legged on the floor, I spread the pages out and scanned the want ads. My eyes caught on one: "Cocktail Waitress Wanted – Prima Donna Jazz Club, Downtown."

A jazz club.

I'd never been a cocktail waitress before, but seeing the ad, I knew that I had to call. I called the number listed, and the voice on the other end invited me to come in for an interview the next day.

The Prima Donna was located in the heart of downtown Portland. When I walked in, it felt like stepping into another world. The lights were dim. The room was empty except for George, the owner and bartender. He was behind the bar, which was a few steps down from the main floor. He was middle-aged with a kind smile and a nice disposition.

"Have you ever been a cocktail waitress before?" he asked.

"No," I admitted, "but I've done a lot of waitressing ... and I learn fast." George gave me a once-over, his smile never fading. He hired me on the spot. "You'll do fine. Can you start tomorrow night?"

"Yes," I said, trying to keep my voice steady. Inside, I was bursting with excitement. "Good. Be here at 7:00 p.m. The band starts at 9:00 p.m.

"Thanks, George, I'll be here!"

The Prima Donna turned out to be the coolest, hippest jazz club in the Pacific Northwest.

The courageous move that I made to leave New York and go to Portland put me right into the music world that I so craved to be in. I showed up the next night in my black skirt and white blouse—the same outfit I'd worn at Marty's in Saratoga Springs. George handed me a little black apron, a cocktail tray, and a bank of cash to make change.

He explained how to put in my orders at the bar, to give customers their drinks, and to make change. He said, "You come over to the bar and cash out at the end of the night after you give "last call" at two. We give "last call" at two, and the club closes at two-thirty. Tips are yours after you balance out."

I was learning as I went along. I was sure that it was going to be a lot easier to carry drinks around on a small cocktail tray than to carry dinners for six around on a gigantic serving tray balanced on my shoulder with one hand and carrying a fold-out stand to open up in the other hand. I'd done that for several years, so I was good at it, but I really didn't want to do that anymore.

I noticed on my drive into Portland around 6:00 p.m. that on my side of the freeway heading south into the city, traffic was "clear sailing" and that on the other side of the freeway, where traffic was headed north, out of the city, it looked like a parking lot. When I'd drive home after work, about 3:00 a.m., there was hardly any traffic. I liked that a lot. I liked not going the same way as everybody else. It was kind of a metaphor for my life. I was following my own path, not anyone else's. I stayed true to myself and didn't care what other people were doing.

On my first night at the Prima Donna, the club was crowded, and the band was playing smokin' hot jazz. A guy came in with a trumpet and sat in with the band. I listened and was stunned by what I heard. The guy played his heart out. His cheeks got real big at times. He was pouring everything that he had in his soul and his entire being into his music.

We gave "last call" at 2:00 a.m., and by 2:30 a.m., everybody had cleared out. After everyone had left, I was cashing out my till with George when he answered the phone. He handed it to me, and much to my surprise, he said, "It's for you." I didn't know anybody in Portland. I'd just gotten there. I didn't have any idea of who it could possibly be. It was the trumpet player.

He told me who he was and that his name was Basil Clark. He wanted to know if I wanted "to go hang out with him." I said, "you're old enough to be my dad. I'd like to hang out with you, but... no funny business...ok?" he agreed and said he'd be over to pick me up.

Basil came to pick me up about 3:00 a.m. The next thing I knew, I was in a car with him, and his driving seemed to defy all laws of gravity and physics as he drove around Portland. He was going the wrong way down one-way streets, driving up on sidewalks and over curbs. We were driving fast and reckless as I sat in the passenger seat, suspended in disbelief. Finally, he drove over a long grass lawn all the way up to the steps of a Denny's a restaurant, where he came to a stop. He stopped his car AT the steps leading to the front doors. We got out of his car, like it was normal, walked up to the doors and went inside. We sat down in a booth. I'd been driving around downtown Portland with a guy who was completely out of his mind.

What a relief to sit down safely in a booth. I felt myself calm down as Basil bought me breakfast. It was 4:00 a.m. Everything seemed so surreal. Basil was a heroin addict, and he was high as a kite. After he ordered breakfast, he started telling me about himself. He told me that he'd just gotten out of prison, where somebody had kicked his teeth out, and he was trying "to get his chops back." I couldn't imagine what his life was like.

He told me that he was a friend and roommate of Chet Baker's. I knew who Chet Baker was. I was a fan of his music. He was also a trumpet player, one of the most well know jazz players. There's a book that's a biography about Chet's life called "Deep in a Dream.. The Long Night of Chet Baker" by James Gavin. I'd read it. In it, it talks about how Chet had also had his teeth kicked out in prison and it talked about a house that Basil mentioned to me that they had shared. Chet was a very famous jazz player, and Basil was also a great talent. They were both heroin addicts, and they both lost their lives to their addiction. Chet got pushed out of a window and fell to his death while he was in London. The book talks about the incident and an investigation that was done. It didn't say much more about it other than they knew that Chet owed money to people for drugs and that that's probably what led to his death.

Basil never came back into the Prima Donna after the wild night that I spent those few hours with him, and I never saw him again. I learned years later from his girlfriend, who I came across on Facebook that Basil had died from an overdose. Like his friend Chet, he was gone too soon. He left me with the memory of a night that I'll never forget.

I heard a lot of great jazz during the few months that I worked at the Prima Donna. I became friends with the regular piano player, an older man named Dick. He was a close friend of an extremely talented young pianist around my age, who I had yet to meet at that time but who I would go on to spend the next eight years with after I left Portland. I wasn't comfortable in Portland. I didn't really know anybody, and I didn't like living alone. The George, who I'd lived with on the coast and in upstate New York, called me and told me that he had found a house to rent on the Oregon Coast and that he was moving back there. He was moving to a town called Lincoln City about 50 north of Yachats, which is about an hour's drive west of Salem, the capital of Oregon, and where Paul, the talented young pianist who'd I'd yet to meet, lived. New York George asked me if I wanted to leave Portland and move in with him in Lincoln City. I said, "OK, George, but only as a roommate." He said that was OK with him. I put in my notice at the Prima Donna and got ready to move to another place that I'd never been to. I moved to Lincoln City.

I met up with George at a house that he rented in Lincoln City. It had two bedrooms and was on a bluff overlooking the coast. I got a job as a waitress at a place called the Rip Tides. I was still twenty-one, maybe twenty-two. I was a food waitress carrying those big trays again, doing the delicate balancing act with a folding stand, and I also took drink orders. The Rip Tides was built on the same bluff as the rental house, overlooking the magnificent Oregon coast.

It had a lounge where we'd put in our drink orders. The bartender would make them, and then we'd take them to our tables while the customers waited for their dinners. There was a band playing in the lounge on the weekends. It was called Paul Painter and Company. Paul was the piano player. He was the guy who was the best friend of the piano player that I'd met at the Prima Dona in Portland and the pianist that I'd go on to become best friends with and spend the next eight years with.

He played in a very flashy style and had a lot of professional experience. He'd had his own television show when he was ten and went on to play in a rock band that was just about to sign with a big label when the whole deal fell apart. He had a big chip on his shoulder about the music business. I learned about all of this after we became friends and I got to know him.

We were about the same age and born in the same month. I started to go in to listen to him play after my shifts and started to talk with him on his breaks. We took an instant liking to each other. We both liked to make each other laugh, and we really got along well. I asked him if he would give me piano lessons. I had saved up enough money and FINALLY bought my first real piano since I'd lost my piano in Yonkers so many years before.

I bought a beautiful, high-quality Decker Brothers upright grand piano. It had a black satin finish, white ivory keys, and black mahogany keys. My life.. like the keys on my new piano, was all lined up again. I was so happy! The piano weighed about 700 pounds. I had it moved into my bedroom at the house that I was sharing with George. I was so excited that I could hardly sleep.

My bed was right across from my piano. I'd wake up all the time at night to look to make sure that it was still really there and that it wasn't just a dream. It had taken so many years of working so hard as a waitress, moving all over the place, from coast to coast, always keeping that picture of my piano teacher in my minds eye to finally, once again, have my beloved piano. Once again, I was at a new beginning. I was excited and happy. I began to pursue my dream with more passion and determination than ever. I was a "girl on fire," as Alicia Keys put it in one of her songs.

I could now begin my journey of becoming a professional pianist and finding my place in the world of music. I would get the education and the experience that I needed. I would have to continue working as a waitress until I didn't have to be a waitress anymore. I could see the light at the end of the tunnel, and it wasn't a train. It was my destiny. I could finally see myself in the picture. I could imagine myself dressed in a beautiful gown, playing concerts. Having that dream for myself was what had kept me going for so many years.

I became friends with Paul's guitar player, Phil. After I'd lived with George for a few months with my 700-pound piano in my bedroom, Phil told me that he was going to be moving out of a nice little house that he was renting a few miles away and that I could move in and take over his lease if I wanted to.

I wanted to! I was able to move out of the house that I had been sharing with beady eyed George and moved into Phil's house as soon as he left. I had my piano moved into the living room and put in the center of the back wall. The other walls had windows that overlooked the coast. It was heaven.

Paul and Phil were my musician friends, and I met a singer named Renee. We liked to laugh, and we all loved music. They'd each come over to visit me. I'd listen to Paul or Phil play and I started to accompany Renee. She was a really good singer. She wound up working in Vegas as a Janis Joplin impersonator for a while.

Paul started giving me piano lessons, and although we did spend the next eight years together, we never lived together. When he gave me lessons, he skipped over all of the fundamentals. He started me out by teaching me a jazz piece called "Blue Bossa" by Kenny Duram. Paul didn't want to teach piano. He was just helping me out. The chords he taught me were really advanced jazz chords that sounded absolutely beautiful. He kept me in a room at a music store all day one time and wouldn't let me out until I could play it. It took me all day for me to learn it. I've never forgotten it. I can still play it. I've played it thousands of times since. It was the first piece that I'd learned on piano since I had taken lessons in New York.

Paul lived in Salem and drove over to play in Lincoln City on the weekends. He told me about a man that he knew named Ed Lais who gave piano lessons in Salem. I drove over to a music store in Salem for Paul to introduce me to Ed. When I walked into the store, Ed was playing a flashy early jazz novelty piece called "Dizzy Fingers." I wanted to learn it! It was a piece that I'd heard Liberace play in his Vegas act. Liberace made it even more flashy. I learned how to play the piece and figured out how to play Liberace's arrangement of it.

I started lessons taking with Ed the week after I met him. I'd make the hour drive over from the coast every week and have lessons with him at his house. He started teaching me how to read music, how to play three-note chords, and all of the basic music fundamentals that I needed to learn.

He let me start working on "Dizzy Fingers," along with my other, more basic assignments. He showed me the chords that it was made out of, how they were played one note at a time in something called arpeggios and, how the patterns repeated, and how they were written in sections. The whole piece is made out of three sections. I was able to understand the music because Ed taught me my chords. Music made sense to me. It was very much like learning a language, and the chords were the words.

He also taught me scales, gave me technical exercises to do and fingered my music for me so that my fingers would become trained. I decided to move to Salem. I could learn music there. It had Ed and Paul, Willamette University, a community college, and a business school. It was the next place for me to go.

I gave my notice at the Rip Tides and moved to Salem. By the time I moved to Salem I had moved seven times after leaving Las Vegas. I'd gone cross country and back, each time moving to a new place that I'd never been to before. This time, I could see that I'd have opportunities that I hadn't had before. I was eager for new opportunities. I really kept at it. I was still waitressing, and I practiced every chance that I got. It was the 3rd time that I'd be moving my 700 lb. piano.

Not Mazzi Material

I answered an ad in the Salem newspaper, and made arrangements to go over to the house and to meet my potential new roommates. The house was hidden away on Larmer Avenue, a quiet street surrounded by warehouses. When I arrived, I couldn't believe my eyes. It was a mansion tucked away in the heart of downtown, with a sprawling lawn and a regal white lion statue guarding the entrance.

Two young women, Mahein and Margie, greeted me at the door. Mahein, a Willamette University student from Iran, was the most exotic and beautiful young woman I'd ever seen. She was the epitome of elegance and warmth. Her eyes sparkled when she spoke, and her easy laughter made me feel instantly welcome. She was smart and fun, and I really liked her. Margie, quieter and reserved, exuded a calm and mature demeanor.

We went into the living room and talked for a while. Mahein did most of the talking.

Together, they showed me through the house—its grand rooms, gleaming kitchen, and the most exquisite bathroom I'd ever seen. I loved it!

After our tour, Mahein and Margie talked for a minute by themselves in the kitchen and then came back to where I was waiting in the living room. After they returned, they offered me the room upstairs; I didn't hesitate. This was where I belonged. I was so happy! I'd found the perfect place and the perfect roommates. I moved in and stayed for the next six years.

The mansion became my haven. My roommates and I settled into an easy and relaxed relationship. Margie loved gardening. She loved to work in the backyard's rose garden, which had the largest roses I've ever seen. It was a vivid tapestry of yellows, reds, and pinks. The scent of freshly cut roses filled the house, blending with the warmth of the friendship that we developed in the beautiful mansion. Mahein made rice with spices and nuts that her family sent from home.

She shared her delicious rice and stories of her home life in Iran. Her dreams for the future inspired me. Together, we created a home that felt like a sanctuary.

Mahein was finishing her final year at the university, Maggie worked a full-time office job, and I attended the local business college and continued to waitress to cover my expenses.

I set up three pianos throughout the house—one in the basement, one in my room, and my 700-pound upright grand in a room off of the kitchen that overlooked the rose garden. I practiced incessantly, pouring every ounce of determination into my dream of becoming a professional pianist. When I wasn't practicing, I was studying. Business school had become my ticket to financial independence. I aced my shorthand classes, mastered bookkeeping and typing, and embraced the confidence that came with the "dress for success" class. I was thrilled the day I received my Nordstrom credit card—a tangible sign of my progress that enabled me to "dress for success."

My financial aid didn't cover everything. I still needed a job to make ends meet.

That's how I found myself at Mazzi's, a bustling Italian restaurant managed by the insufferable Randy. The staff tolerated his delusions of grandeur, but his condescending attitude grated on all of us who worked for him. The restaurant was always packed, and the tips were decent. For a while, it worked.

When Mazzi's closed for six weeks to remodel, my financial situation got tight. I had to sell my beloved Fuji bicycle—a gift from Paul—to pay my rent. Losing the bike was heartbreaking, a painful reminder of how precarious my financial situation was. Paul was ever supportive and understood, but the loss and the embarrassment of having to sell it to pay my rent and having to tell him weighed heavily on me.

During those six weeks, I discovered the practice rooms at Willamette University. Paul had shown me the music building, and it quickly became my refuge. The rooms, each equipped with a piano, were rarely used. I spent hours there, sometimes playing late into the night, the sound of my music filling the empty halls. It was here that I found solace and honed my craft, working feverishly on scales and finger exercises and the promise of what could be.

When Mazzi's reopened, I drove out in my snappy red and white Toyota Corolla that my mom was able to buy for me during the closure. It was the first time that I'd ever received any financial help from my family since I'd moved out on my own when I was seventeen. I had a little yellow car that Paul wanted me to buy. He was going to "soup it up" for me, but the engine fell out of it. My mom's help came just in time, and I found the perfect car for the exact amount of money that she was able to send me.

When I drove out to check the schedule, I discovered that my name missing. I found Randy and said, "Randy, I don't see my name of the schedule?" he smirked as he said, "I've decided that you're not "Mazzi material." His words stung, not just for their cruelty but for the abruptness with which he dismissed me. I sat in disbelief. I repeated what I'd heard in my mind,

"I'm not Mazzi Material?" The words echoed in my head as I sat there, stunned. I didn't move. I needed a moment for what he said to sink in. Randy had the spirit of the original "mean girl"—cutting, smug, and intentional.

After a few minutes, an idea sparked. I got up and walked into the bar where Dick, the owner, was working. "Hi, Dick. Can I talk to you for a minute?" He said, "Sure." "Have you ever thought about having live music in the bar?" I asked. He looked intrigued. "I could bring my Rhodes piano and play on the weekends. It might be nice for the customers to have music to listen to while they wait for their tables." After a moment's consideration, he agreed. We agreed on how much I would be paid and that I would start that weekend.

Paul helped me set up my Rhodes in the lounge, and I played my heart out. The customers loved it, and Dick was thrilled. That was the last time that I ever worked as a waitress! and it was my first job as a musician, a pianist! Randy, who had intended to be mean, had done me the biggest favor ever! The lounge was filled with the sound of familiar standards and pop arrangements. My music created a relaxing and intimate atmosphere. People stayed all night. I loved watching people arrive, sometimes seeming tense, and by the end of the evening, they were relaxed and happy. My tip jar was full and my playing was a big success! ..the feeling of walking by Randy on my way to the lounge was one of sheer joy. I'd smile at him and give him a little sideways wave, like the Queen.

A few weeks in, a saxophonist and singer named Lee joined me. He was a seasoned performer, his soulful voice and skilled playing elevating our act. Together, we developed a following, filling the lounge with regulars who came to enjoy our music. Lee negotiated better pay for us, and I soaked up everything I could from him, learning new tunes and refining my style.

Playing at Mazzi's marked the true beginning of my professional musical career and the end of my waitressing career. My confidence grew with each performance. Mazzi's had closed one door, but it had opened another—one that led straight to my dreams.

Finally, It Was Me in the Picture!

I was far along enough in my program at business school that I was given an option to work and get school credit if I could find a job in business during my last semester. I would still have to take all of my finals and a few classes, but there were other classes that I wouldn't have to take. I found a part time day job as a secretary working at a newspaper. I worked at the newspaper a few hours a week, continued with my business school classes, played at Mazzi's on the weekends, and continued to practice at Willamette every chance that I got. I stayed focused and was very driven. I was in those practice rooms every day, no matter how tired I was or how long my day had been. Even with three pianos at home to use to practice on, I preferred the practice rooms at Willamette. It felt like it was the right place for me to be, and it turned out that it was.

If I hadn't kept showing up there to practice at Willamette, what happened next never would have happened.

I had become friends with Sarah, a vibes player from Sacramento who was a student at Willamette. We started practicing together in the band room, where she kept her vibraphone. One day, while I was warming up before Sarah arrived, a professor walked in. It was Professor Benhke, the director of Willamette's two jazz bands. He needed a piano player for one of them. After listening to me play, he asked, "Would you like to join the jazz band?"

I didn't hesitate. "I'd LOVE to!"

I was placed in Ensemble II—the group for less experienced players—which suited me perfectly. I didn't mention that I wasn't a student or that I couldn't read music very well.

Rehearsals started that week. I showed up excited and nervous, clutching the folder of music that was handed to me. As I scanned the pages, relief washed over me—a lot of it looked familiar, like the chord charts I'd seen in the Real Book, something that I was very familiar with. But some parts were fully written out, and I knew I'd need help. Sarah and I practiced together, and I worked my way through the tricky parts bit by bit.

Professor Benhke was a hands-on leader. He pointed at us randomly during rehearsals, signaling who should take a solo. When it was my turn, I just went for it—making things up on the spot, feeling my way through the chords and rhythm. Professor Benhke always seemed pleased.

The concert was scheduled for six weeks later. I poured every ounce of energy I had into rehearsing, substituting the more advanced jazz voicings that I was more familiar with where I could. When the big night arrived, Professor Benhke surprised me: he put my picture on the cover of the concert program. Finally, after so many years of imagining it, it truly was ME in the picture! Sitting at the grand piano on stage, with the lights warm and bright, felt like a dream. The music flowed, and the audience rewarded us with a standing ovation. I didn't want the night to end.

WILLAMETTE UNIVERSITY
Presents

— *JAZZ NIGHT* —

THE WILLAMETTE UNIVERSITY
Jazz Ensemble I
and
Jazz Ensemble II

Wednesday   December 2, 1981

8:00 p.m. — Smith Auditorium

A picture of the concert brochure courtesy
of Willamette University

A few days after our concert, Professor Benhke asked to see me in his office. Nervously, I walked in, thinking that he'd found out that I wasn't a student and that I might be in some trouble.

Instead, he looked at me, smiled, and said, "Congratulations on your fine performance. I'm really proud of how well the band did. We had a great night!" I smiled and said, "it was wonderful." He then looked at me and said, "you can't read music, can you?"

Embarrassed, I looked down at my shoes as I answered, "no." What he said next changed my life.

He said, "with enough training and hard work, I believe that you could become "the next Marian McPartland."

Marian McPartland was my idol! My hero. I could barely breathe as his words sank in. Then came the final shock: he told me that he had arranged for me to play an audition for Willamette University. I was overwhelmed and felt tears of joy welling up inside. He told me to prepare three pieces for my audition and that my audition would be in about three weeks.

I threw myself into preparing for my audition. I chose "Dizzy Fingers," a flashy novelty piece I'd learned from Ed Lais, and two Bach Preludes I'd taught myself. I practiced relentlessly, determined to show up ready.

Then disaster struck.

Four days before my audition, while opening a can with a hand-held can opener, I slipped. The lid sliced through the top of my thumb on my right hand, nearly severing it. Blood poured everywhere. I wrapped it in a towel and called out to my roommate, Wendy. She came into the kitchen and saw what had happened.

"Wendy! Can you drive me to the hospital?" I asked, panicking.

"No," she said, backing away. "I can't handle it."

She left me standing in the kitchen. I had no choice but to drive myself to the hospital—with a stick shift. How I managed it, I'll never know.

At the emergency room, they stitched my thumb and wrapped it in a big white bandage. I was given painkillers and sent home. My audition was on Thursday.

I didn't cancel. I couldn't. I wouldn't.

On the morning of the audition, I stood before a panel of four professors, including Professor Benhke. My thumb, wrapped like a mummy, throbbed as I walked to the grand piano.

"Are you ready?" Professor Benhke asked.

I smiled, gave a small bow, and sat at the piano. I took a deep breathe and began.

The pain hit hard halfway through "Dizzy Fingers." My thumb started to bleed, and tears welled up. I didn't stop. I couldn't. I gasped for air between sobs, the music becoming raw and imperfect, but I pressed on. I don't remember how much more I played. I know that I made it as far as one of the Bach Preludes.

Finally, Professor Benhke came up to me, put his hands gently on my shoulders, and said, "You can stop now."

He smiled and told me to wait outside. I sat on the grass, leaning against a tree on the lawn, tears streaming down my face, clutching my aching thumb.

A few minutes later, Professor Benhke walked out with a big smile. He looked at me and said, "Welcome to the university!"

With those words, my life changed forever. I was granted a Talent Award Scholarship. I was officially a music student at the University!

It was the end of the school year. I would start my music studies and private lessons at Willamette in the fall. I called my mom and my Uncle

Eddie. They were both overjoyed. My uncle offered to pay my rent while I would be attending school. He understood our shared love of music and saw that I was following in his footsteps. I was his legacy. I felt his pride in my determination to follow my own path in my own musical journey, inspired by his.

Paul congratulated me on receiving the scholarship, but his excitement seemed subdued. He said something about ensuring my success if I stayed with him, but I didn't understand what he meant.

Balancing my two jobs, practicing, and studying for finals stretched me to the limit. Paul grew frustrated with my lack of time for him, and one evening, while I was buried in books, he gave me an ultimatum: agree to marry him, or he'd leave. I was so busy studying and working at the time that what he said didn't sink in. By the time finals were over, he was gone.

When I walked in the door and showed up at the Monday night jam session, he played the tune "Just Friends" as a new woman sauntered past me. The way she tossed her hair as she walked by me sent me the signal that he had moved on. My heart shattered. I begged him to come back, but he refused. The weight of the loss was immense, but I had to carry on.

Fall semester at Willamette was everything I'd hoped for. Music theory, solfeggio, private lessons, and jazz band filled my days. I kept playing at Mazzi's and added a part-time office job to make ends meet. My boss adored me, even though my typewriting mishaps filled the trash can with crumpled paper. It took me forever to type a letter without any mistakes. At that time, if you made a mistake, you had to take out the paper, throw it away, and start again.

One day, I wandered into a lounge across the street from my office and landed a gig playing and singing a few nights a week. Combined with my other jobs, I was making over $700 a week—more money than I'd ever made. But the workload was unsustainable. I was exhausted. After finishing my business degree, I gave my notice at my office job.

My boss was very surprised and disappointed. I knew that working in an office wasn't going to be my lifetime career. Music was my future, and I'd achieved my goal of never having to waitress again.

James, a trumpet player from Seattle, began sitting in at the Boone's jam sessions. He recognized my ambition and encouraged me to transfer to an arts college in Seattle. "If you want to become a professional, Salem isn't the place to do it," he said. "You're going to have to move to Seattle. There's an arts college there. I can get you an audition."

The idea of leaving Salem was daunting. Willamette had become home, and Seattle was a sprawling, unfamiliar city. But after losing Paul, staying in Salem felt unbearable. James drove me to Seattle to play an audition that he had arranged for me at the arts college.

When we got there, he eased the car to a stop at the curb. I got out of his car and gazed up at the building. From the outside, it seemed impressive, with its stately facade and neatly trimmed lawn. But stepping inside, the illusion faded quickly. The lobby looked worn and had a musty smell. The space lacked the charm of the exterior. My nerves tightened.

Crossing the worn wooden floor, I spotted a counter staffed by a few people. On my way, I passed office doors slightly ajar, revealing cluttered desks and faded posters. I approached the counter, the echo of my footsteps filling the quiet lobby.

"I'm here for an audition with the music department," I said, my voice steadier than I felt.

The woman behind the counter nodded and pointed toward the stairs. "Second floor. Room at the end of the hall."

The staircase creaked faintly underfoot as I climbed. The hall on the second floor was narrow, its walls lined with doors. Finding the designated room, I paused, smoothed my clothes, and knocked lightly.

"Come in," a voice called.

Inside, a man sat at a desk near a large window that bathed the room in pale light. There were two grand pianos in the room. The man didn't rise to greet me; his demeanor was nonchalant, almost indifferent.

"I'm here for the audition," I said, smiling nervously. He barely nodded, motioning toward one of the pianos.

"Go ahead," he said curtly.

I took my place at the piano. I had prepared meticulously, pouring weeks of effort into my arrangement of Charlie Parker's "Donna Lee." I was auditioning for the jazz department, so I chose one of the most challenging and iconic pieces. My fingers hovered over the keys before diving into the melody. I played it in unison two octaves apart. It's a particularly hard piece to finger for the piano, having been written by Charlie Parker, a legendary saxophone player. The fast-paced bebop tune demanded precision and energy. I moved through the piece after playing the melody, improvising in my right hand while maintaining a steady walking bass line with my left. Chords punctuated the rhythm, adding texture and color.

Halfway through my improvisation, the man's voice broke in. "You're in." I stopped, unsure if I'd heard correctly.

"That's enough," he added, waving me off. That was a shock to hear, mixed with confusion. Was that all? "Head downstairs to the financial aid office and make arrangements," he instructed. A mix of triumph and bewilderment swirled within me. I hadn't even finished, yet somehow, I was accepted.

Before heading to financial aid, I asked, "Will I always have access to good practice pianos?" the question burning in my mind.

The man barely looked up. "You'll get a key to the second-floor practice rooms. The pianos there will always be available to you."

With his assurance and his promise, I descended the stairs and entered the financial aid office. The counselor guided me through the paperwork for grants, loans, and my transfer.

I told the counselor that I would need to start working as soon as I moved to Seattle during the summer, a few months before school started. I inquired about the Talent Bank which had music jobs for students.

"There's a bulletin board in the hallway," he said. "You'll find summer job postings there. The talent bank won't be up until after the semester starts."

I found the bulletin board and scanned it for a summer job. I found an ad for a demolition crew at the south campus. Demolition? The term was unfamiliar, but I jotted down the number and made the call. The voice on the other end confirmed I could start as soon as I arrived in Seattle. I wasn't sure what it was, but it was a job, so I took it.

Back in Salem, I shared my plans with Sarah, the vibes player. We unfolded a paper map of Washington on the living room floor, tracing routes and studying Seattle's layout. Without cell phones or the internet, the map was our only guide to navigating the Seattle area.

Sarah decided to take over my place in the beautiful house, agreeing to handle the rent payments. The arrangement felt bittersweet. This house had been my haven, a place of growth and discovery, that I loved, but it was time to move on in my journey.

James offered his help, volunteering to drive me to Seattle and to let me stay at his house there temporarily. He was returning to his hometown after leaving his job at the music store in Salem. His support steadied me as I prepared for the leap.

Saying goodbye to my professors at Willamette was the hardest part. I thanked them for their guidance and became a little emotional as I explained my decision. Their encouragement stayed with me as I sold my beloved Decker Brothers piano and packed up my belongs, each box a reminder of the journey I was leaving behind and the uncertain road ahead. With a deep breath, I embraced the courage it would take to start anew.

Moving with James
to Seattle

The day came when it was time to leave Salem. James arrived in his VW bus.

Sarah had helped me pack my things into boxes. Together, we loaded everything into James's VW bus. He carefully hoisted my Rhodes piano into the back, ensuring it was secure. With everything packed, we left Salem behind, the familiar streets disappearing in the rearview mirror. Six hours later, we pulled into his neighborhood on Beacon Hill in Seattle. The late-July sun cast long shadows over the small, older homes perched on steep hills, each accessible by equally steep concrete stairs.

James's house was modest, on top a hill, with its own steep set of cement stairs leading up to the front door. Next door, his parents lived in a similar home. After introducing me to them, James and I returned to his house. His mother, absorbed in watching the Olympics, had barely managed a tearful hello, too emotional to chat. Back at James's, he assured me he'd take me to show me how to drive to school the next day.

The following morning, we set out for Capitol Hill. As James drove, he pointed out landmarks and explained the route. The streets of Beacon Hill gave way to older apartment buildings, and the closer we got to Capitol Hill, the livelier it became. Small ethnic restaurants lined the roads, their colorful signs competing for attention. People bustled about, a mix of families, students, and a distinct group dressed in black— tight jeans, leather jackets, spiked mohawk haircuts, with black hair and makeup. It was my first glimpse of Seattle's punk and goth scene, a striking contrast to Salem's quiet streets.

Capitol Hill had an edgy vibrancy, but it also felt chaotic. We passed loud, lively gay bars and groups of tattooed and pierced individuals. James pointed out the main school building and the south campus, just down the street, where my summer job would be. Though the area had its charms, I couldn't shake a sense of unease. It was a completely unfamiliar place.

The next morning, I drove myself to the South campus start my demolition job. I was there at 8:00 a.m. There was a parking lot at that campus. I parked and went inside. The first floor was empty, and there wasn't any electricity on. I climbed the stairs to the second floor as instructed. It looked like a bomb had gone off. One entire wall was gone. There was a huge gaping hole. There was nothing between me and the other people there and the outdoors. Through the gaping hole, I could see my car parked below. Oh my gosh! This was the job that I'd signed up for!

The noise was deafening—drills, sledgehammers, and crashing debris. The air was thick and full of clouds of grey dust, making it hard to breathe. I was the only female. A guy approached me and handed me a five-gallon bucket. "Your job is to pick up the pieces of CONCRETE from the walls we're knocking out, fill the bucket, and dump it out through that hole." None of the guys working there were wearing hard hats or dust masks, and nobody gave me any protective gear.

I didn't know what to do. I filled up the bucket with pieces of concrete but couldn't lift it. No one came over to lift it for me, so I removed most of the pieces of concrete until I could drag the bucket to the edge and dump it out of the gaping hole onto a big pile two stories below. The day felt endless. Somehow, I lasted a whole day. I knew that there was no way that I was ever going back there again. By the time I left, I was covered in ash-colored dust, my muscles ached, and I felt as miserable as I looked. I drove back to James's house, took a shower, and went to bed. I was exhausted. The next morning, instead of going back to the demolition job, I went straight to the financial aid office and explained my situation. "Can you please find me another job? I have a two-year business degree, and I can't do manual labor on a demolition crew."

The counselor nodded sympathetically. "We have a work-study position available at an architect's office nearby. Interested?"

"Yes! Absolutely."

He handed me the contact information. I called as soon as I got back to James' house. I got an interview for the next day. I got dressed in a beautiful skirt and top with a white business jacket that I'd bought for my "dress for success" class. I went over for my interview at an architect's office on Denny Way, probably the steepest hill in Seattle but close to school. The two Harvard-educated architects who owned the firm were kind and professional. After a brief interview, they hired me on the spot.

The job was a perfect fit. My main tasks included answering phones, transferring calls, and typing documents. Unlike the old typewriter I'd struggled with in Salem, the office had a word processor. Fixing mistakes was a breeze. I could type 55 wpm. I could fix mistakes as fast as I could type them. My efficiency made me look like a typing whiz.

The work-study hours accommodated my school schedule, and the office was only a few blocks from campus, so I could walk to my job from school.

After a few weeks at James' house, he helped me find a room in the "U District" near the University of Washington. The house, owned by his friend Keith, was far from ideal. Keith had crammed six tenants into a four-bedroom house. My room was an unfinished basement bedroom. He'd turned the basement into two additional unfinished bedrooms. I shared the basement with another tenant, Shelley. Upstairs, the other four roommates included three students: a sweet girl named Natalie, an Asian student, and a pianist who ran the music department at the UW. There was also a young woman named Tiger who dressed a leotard outfit, and no one really knew what she did, other than live there. She stayed to herself a lot and occasionally has some male visitors. The environment was crowded and somewhat chaotic, but it was a start.

Parking at school was a nightmare, and so was parking at the house. There wasn't a parking lot for students at school. That meant that you had to parallel park, circling blocks until you found a spot. Cars were usually parked about an inch away from each other with some of their wheels up on the curbs. Sometimes, the spots were blocks away from school, and you'd have to walk with your books, often in the rain, from wherever you were lucky enough to find a spot.

At Keith's house, street cleaning schedules forced us to move our cars constantly.

Seattle's urban quirks took some getting used to. I had to make huge adjustments. The only thing that I could do was to hang in there, move forward, and do whatever I could to make things work. I often reminded myself that this was the price of pursuing my dream.

Fortunately, the school's talent bank was great. They began getting me steady music jobs. I played elegant private parties, fundraisers, weddings, and events for Seattle's elite. Introducing myself as the pianist from the Arts College always garnered respect, and the grand pianos at these venues made the performance a joy. I learned to adapt quickly—pausing for speeches, adjusting to requests, and ensuring the music fit the occasion. Each job taught me valuable lessons about professionalism and adaptability. I enjoyed that experience very much, and the pay was very good. I got a $500.00 tip one night.

However, the rest of my experience at the College was disappointing. The school was disorganized. Many of the teachers prioritized their careers over their students. The head of the music department, who I'd auditioned for, was particularly unhelpful. Some of the teachers often canceled classes without notice, the classes were often disorganized, and the programs weren't well organized... One teacher would just leave a post-it note on the door saying that class had been cancelled whenever he couldn't make it. The high tuition felt increasingly unjustifiable.

One humiliating incident was, understandably, an unacceptable frustration. I'd prepared for a solo concert in the auditorium, inviting friends and colleagues. When they arrived, the doors were locked. I couldn't get into the back stage area to prepare, and my friends were locked outside in the hallway. Frantic, I sought help from the music department head, but he shrugged off my concerns, saying that he couldn't help. Embarrassed, I had to send everyone home without performing.

Despite these setbacks at school, I found a better place to live. Two of my roommates from Keith's house and I moved to a quieter, safer home still in the U District, but much nicer. Leaving behind the chaos of Tiger and the cramped conditions made life much better, and parking was much easier.

As the semester ended, I faced an end of the semester performance—a final project requiring me to assemble a band and perform for a panel. I recruited a talented guitarist named Rich, whom I'd met months earlier when he offered to help me carry some gear into the school. Along with a bassist and drummer, we formed a quartet.

Our performance went well. The other members of my band left, and the adjudicators, who were teachers in the music department and the guy who was the head of it, made comments to me after they left. One of them told me that I had a great voice but that my singing a little flat, something that the "world-renowned" vocal teacher that I'd been taking a vocal class from never mentioned.

Then there was the head of the music department. Yes, same the same guy who I had auditioned for, who had cut my audition short, quickly accepted me into the music department and didn't care that I was locked out of the auditorium to play my concert. He criticized my selection of tunes. He said, "we're not here to listen to your lounge act."

We had rehearsed and put on a nice performance. The only reason that they were listening to my "lounge act" tunes was because so far in the two years that I'd been a student there, I hadn't learned one new song that I could use for my end of he semester performance. I'd always been an A student in excellent schools, and here I was in a sub- standard school, getting C's. It was the end of the semester and summer break. I didn't know if I'd be back...especially after what happened next.

I went over to school to practice when summer break began. The music department head PROMISED me after I auditioned for him that I would ALWAYS be able to use the good pianos in the practice rooms on the second floor. He didn't do anything to make sure that I had a new key after the locks were changed for summer break. I went to practice and couldn't get into any of the rooms. He was unavailable to reach at school. The office gave me his home number, so I called him at home.

He was annoyed that I'd called him at home. I explained the problem and asked him to get me a key. He actually said, "at first, I thought that you might be trouble. Now I see that you're just a pain in the ass." I was shocked.. but given his past behavior and his indifference, I wasn't surprised. He then suggested that I use the University of Washington's facilities instead. That was unbelievable. I was a hardworking student struggling to pay the high tuition, sleeping on the floor of my bedroom in our apartment to afford to pay the tuition. That did it for me. He made my decision to leave for me. I knew that the Arts college was a waste of time and money and that it was time for me to start looking for my way out. It was time to get out of the quicksand that I kept feeling I was sinking further and further into, piling up student loans.

I actually did wind up having to go to the University of Washington to use their practice rooms. I had to walk several blocks from our apartment over to the UW music building. I would often return late at night. It was a dangerous place to be walking around alone and, especially dangerous at night.

I told Rich about my problem of not having a safe place to practice, about being locked out of the practice rooms at school, and about having been told to go to the UW to use their practice rooms. He offered me a safe place to practice at his mobile home about twenty miles north of Seattle. He had an upright piano there.

I'd get to his place before he'd leave for work, playing in bands at night clubs. He'd be gone until two or three in the morning. He liked my playing and my singing and he'd often challenge me to learn a pop tune by ear, using his record player, while he was gone at work.

I'd be able to play it and sing it and have a chart written out for it by the time he'd get home. He was impressed, and he'd often play the tune with me. It was fun.

He taught me more than anybody else ever had about how to work as a professional musician. He taught me about playing three-note chords rather than the jazz chords that I was trying to put into pop tunes, that didn't work. He showed me what did work and how to play in different styles.

He bought me sets of instructional tapes to teach me to play the different styles that I would need to know how to play to be able to work. I learned how to play rock, country, and R&B styles, and he helped me learn what was called "Top 40" and cover tunes.

I was still working a few days a week at the architect's office when I got a call from Ben, a piano player I'd met at school. He had a regular job playing at a restaurant in Kirkland, just outside Seattle, and I occasionally subbed for him. "Hey," he said, "I got offered a job to play on a cruise ship going to Alaska, but I can't do it. Want the audition?"

A cruise ship going to Alaska? The idea sounded like a golden opportunity —playing piano in a swanky lounge while the scenery glided by. I said, "I'd love to!" I nailed the audition, and a week later, I got the call. "You're hired," the man said. My heart leapt. This was my first big step toward building my professional career.

I went to the Society Expeditions office in Everett, just north of Seattle, to finalize the paperwork. When I got to their office, I met a man sitting behind a desk and mentioned how excited I was to be going to "Alaska! He paused, giving me a puzzled look. Alaska?"You think you're going to Alaska?"

He had me follow him over to a wall that had a floor-to-ceiling map of the world on it. He pointed to Alaska and then moved his hand further up. All the way up to the top of the map... to the top of the world. "The ship you will be playing on is not a cruise ship going to Alaska. You'll be playing on board the World Discoverer. It's an expedition going to the Northwest Passage to do research and exploration in the high Arctic during a three-week trip." "An expedition?" I asked, blinking.

I didn't know anything about the high Arctic or about its long, dark history of the ships and the explorers who had gone there before.. and never returned.

The man gave me a minute to think it over.

Somehow, the idea of playing on board an *expedition* didn't quite sink in. I was so excited that I'd won the audition and that I was going to get paid $1,200.00 to play by myself onboard a ship. I was a twenty-seven-year-old music student. This would be my first big step toward building my professional career. Expedition or not, this was still a chance to play music professionally on board a ship. Who knew what kind of new opportunities playing on a ship might bring? I was excited and said, "Yes, I'd like to go!"

After signing the contract, I was given the itinerary. "You'll be leaving in about a week." The man mentioned something about flying to Edmonton, then onward to a small northern town where I'd board the ship. I didn't catch all the details; my mind was already racing, thinking about what music I would bring and what clothes I would take.

The man gave me a big new bright red parka jacket, a big pair of men's big rubber boots and a pair of log dark blue mittens. "These are all insulated to 30 degrees below zero. Be sure and bring some warm clothes. You'll have to fit everything that you're going to take into a backpack." A backpack?... He handed me a 125-page "Expedition Notebook" that has a dark grey heavy stock paper cover, filled with information about the region with pictures of our proposed route. I figured I'd read it after I got on board the ship.

The Northwest Passage Expedition

As soon as I got home, I packed and repacked my backpack several times, carefully considering what music, clothes, and personal items I'd bring. Two black cocktail dresses, heels for performing, makeup, and warm clothes managed to fit alongside my Real Book—a lifeline of over 300 standards and cocktail piano tunes that would carry me through the journey.

Rich treated me to breakfast before dropping me off at Sea-Tac Airport. From there, I joined a group heading to Edmonton, Canada, before meeting the rest of the expedition team at a lounge in our Edmonton motel. It wasn't hard to spot them—identical red parka jackets stood out like we were gearing up for a superhero team-up.

The next day, we flew to Resolute Bay, a frozen outpost at the northern end of the Northwest Passage with a population of about 198. The airport, tiny and isolated, greeted us with a brisk three degrees below zero. I was grateful for the bright red parka now wrapped around me.

In warmed vans, we were driven to the dock where the SS World Discoverer waited. As we approached, excitement buzzed through the group, but I couldn't shake a surreal, Twilight Zone-esque feeling creeping over me. Everything felt oddly cinematic, like stepping into an elaborate film location.

Once aboard, the ship's activities director—cheery, mustached, and quintessentially British—welcomed us warmly. After showing me to my cabin, he casually mentioned that in addition to being the ship's pianist, I'd also be fulfilling crew member duties. Crew member duties? Oh boy, that was news.

My cabin wasn't on the passenger level of the ship. It was a room located all by itself on the main level. It had a single bed, a thick-glassed window, and just enough room for the essentials. It had a small closet off to the right as soon as you entered the room. You had to enter the room and close the door to open the closet door. I unpacked, showered, and donned one of my cocktail dresses for my debut in the ship's lounge.

The lounge was an odd but charming blend of rugged and elegant—there was a short studio upright piano bolted to the floor in the corner of the room and a beautifully crafted wooden bar that looked like it belonged in an old-fashioned high-end saloon at the entrance. I introduced myself to the staff behind the bar and then walked over to the piano. I sat down and began to play as the passengers filtered in, enjoying their drinks and appetizers. I became more relaxed as I played. The music flowed, and I found solace in its familiarity.

The dining room later that night was a revelation, with its grandeur rivaling the Waldorf Astoria. It took me a while to grasp the concept of a "palate cleanser" during dinner—what I mistook for dessert was actually sherbet meant to reset our taste buds. It was embarrassing, but I played it off with a nod of .. "oh, of course...a palate cleanser."

The following day brought our first iceberg sighting—a massive, skyscraper-like presence that dwarfed the size of our ship. It was both awe-inspiring and humbling. Later, we passed by ice floes with polar bears on them, their presence a stark reminder of the untamed wilderness we were now part of.

The ship's library became a sanctuary, where I started to learn about the grim histories of Arctic explorers like John Franklin—the man who infamously ate his boots to survive. Lady Jane Franklin, his remarkable wife, had even ventured into the Arctic at the age of 78 to search for him. Their stories, steeped in resilience and tragedy, were both captivating and haunting.

We would be taking excursions in a Zodiac, a large black inflatable raft, to visit frozen islands in the area. One of our trips would be to Beechey Island, where the I'll-fated Franklin expedition had spent a winter and lost three crew members.

Our first zodiac excursion was a crash course in Arctic exploration. The icy waters and biting wind made the bumpy ten-minute ride through the sea ice feel like an eternity. When we reached the barren, frozen island, I wanted to stretch my legs, and without fully grasping the dangers, I wandered off. Within minutes, the stark realization of my isolation hit me. The sight of the vast, empty Arctic around me was haunting. Hurrying back to the group, I was met with sharp reprimands from a crew member, who explained the rules I had just broken: No one was allowed to venture out of sight of the group or to leave an area after we got out of the Zodiac until a scout had gone to the highest spot on the frozen island and fired a shot into the air to signal that it was safe for us to walk around - that no polar bears had been spotted.

That day's excursion was brief, a trial run. The frozen island felt otherworldly. Silver clouds loomed overhead, blending seamlessly with the horizon-less expanse. The high Arctic was vast and majestic and silent. The only sound that I heard was that of frozen pebbles crunching under my gigantic, insulated men-sized boots.

After another bumpy ride through the sea ice, we returned to the ship. Relief washed over me as we returned to the ship's relative safety. I had only just learned earlier that day that my duties as a crew member included not just assisting passengers with their life jackets but accompanying them on every trip... yes. I was going too. I wasn't sure why.

After I returned to my cabin, I showered, slipped into a cocktail dress, and played piano in the lounge, letting the music soothe my nerves.

The next day, we gathered in the lecture room for a briefing on polar bear safety. These weren't the lazy creatures that I'd seen lounging on rocks at the Bronx zoo—they were swift, starving predators capable of smelling prey from miles away and able to charge at speeds up to 30 mph. The Arctic's dangers were becoming all too real.

I was happy to have a few days onboard the ship between excursions, which brought its own rhythm. I played piano in the lounge, where the music provided calming atmosphere amid the Arctic's raw, untamed beauty. I got to socialize with the passengers—marine biologists, geologists, researchers, Arctic enthusiasts, two wealthy Russian tourists, and a few photographers from National Geographic. Each one had paid $30,000 for this three-week odyssey through the Northwest Passage. Meanwhile, I was just a pianist who thought she'd landed a great gig.

Our next zodiac adventure was to Beechey Island, also known as "the island of lost explores." The passengers were very excited about visiting Beechey Island. It has a special historical significance. Franklin and his men had "over wintered" there, and three of them were were buried in permafrost graves. No one had been there in the previous one hundred and fifty years except for one group of searchers who had been there four years before us, and one them died there. The Franklin expedition bodies were exhumed and taken back. There are pictures of them on the internet. They're pretty scary pictures. It was a place steeped in bleak history, a haunting reminder of the Arctic's unforgiving nature.

The ride to Beechey Island was another bone-rattling journey through sea ice. This time, we followed protocol, staying close together until the scout fired the signal shot. Only then did we cautiously begin to explore. The four white wooden crosses marking the burial site stood stark against the frozen landscape. The cabin ruins and tin cans scattered around, all frozen in time were relics of a desperate attempt to survive.

The eerie silence enveloped us. The only sound was the crunch of pebbles beneath our boots. Paul Simon's "The Sound of Silence" took on a new meaning as I stood still, listening to my own breathing against the Arctic's vast emptiness. It was hauntingly beautiful—and deeply unsettling.

When it was time to leave, we loaded back into the zodiac. A headcount confirmed everyone was present, and we made the wild, icy ride back to the ship. This wasn't the Alaska cruise I had imagined— it was an odyssey into the unknown. And though challenges loomed, a sense of adventure stirred within me as we delved further into the Arctic wilderness.

The days onboard, between excursions, the ship offered a reprieve. There were lectures, historical films, and time spent in the observation room, where thick glass windows framed the icy expanse. Some nights, the Northern Lights illuminated the lounge windows with cascading colors of green, pink, and scarlet. Their beauty washed over the entire sky. It looked like the whole world was bathed in their magnificent swirling colors that were awe-inspiring.

We visited more frozen islands, each uniquely desolate. Sometimes, after an excursion, we'd gather in the ship's cozy library. With books lining the walls from floor to ceiling, it became a place for discovery and conversation. There were comfortable upholstered chairs to sit in and a big rectangular table with chairs with desk lamps where we would show the geologists whatever rocks that we could fit into our pockets that they'd asked us to pick up. The geologists would examine them and show us the fossils that they contained. Some of them had tiny pieces of parts of white shells, and others had little plant-like outlines that were imprinted on them. We'd marvel at their millions of years of history. They were some of the earliest life forms on earth.

In the observation room, passengers mingled or stepped onto the deck to witness the sea ice, polar bears drifting by on ice floes, and towering icebergs. It was a surreal experience, both exhilarating and humbling. I often thought of Ben, the pianist who had passed on this job to me. What I had imagined as a straightforward Alaska cruise had turned into a life-altering Arctic expedition— one I could only hope to survive.

A New Danger - Meeting the Captain

After we returned from Beechey Island, we had another few days at sea. During those days, the captain occasionally came into the lounge to have drinks. His presence transformed the atmosphere. The room quieted as if everyone collectively held their breath. Our lives and the success of this treacherous journey rested in his hands. He was revered as a "god-like" figure by many of the passengers.

The captain was a tall man in his late forties with sandy-colored hair, fit and commanding in his white military uniform adorned with shoulder stripes. His heavy German accent added to his authoritative presence. I'd seen him a few times in the hallways late at night, sometimes accompanied by a woman who was married to a rich Canadian beer mogul.

One evening, while I was playing in the lounge, the captain sent someone over to ask me to join him at his table. Improvising a graceful ending to the song I was playing, I walked over. He motioned for me to sit, and I obliged. His initial small talk was seemingly harmless - a general conversation. He made comments about the northern lights, the passengers' enjoyment of the trip, and whether I was having a good time. The din of cocktail conversations around us made his thick accent harder to follow, but I smiled and nodded politely.

Then, the conversation took a darker turn. His grin shifted into something unsettling as he leaned closer and said, "One night, I will come to visit you in your cabin. You will not know which night." He leaned back, laughing as if he found his own words amusing, but there was no mistaking his intent. I took it for what it was. It was a threat, and I felt a chill run through me.

I excused myself as soon as I could, returning to the piano and later retreating to my cabin. Locking the door, I scanned the small room, searching for anything that could fortify the door or that I could use to defend myself. The stark reality settled in—if the captain had a master key, the lock was meaningless. In that moment, I realized that if he came for me, I would be as vulnerable as prey to a polar bear.

I knew that had to do something to make some kind of a plan and talk to somebody.

The next day, I sat at a table with the Russian couple who I had befriended. They were sitting in a booth, having some food. I sat down with them and wanted to tell them about what the captain had said to me in the lounge, but instead, it was them who had something to tell me: our ship had become stuck in the ice. There was a meeting taking place in the lecture hall and we needed to go to for a briefing.

The lecture hall buzzed with tension as passengers gathered. The activities director, now serving as an expedition guide, informed us that we were immobilized in the Arctic sea ice. A Canadian icebreaker was en route to free us, but it would take a few days to arrive. We were reassured that the ship had ample supplies and that operations on board would continue as usual. Still, the sight of unyielding ice all around us was unnerving. We could hear the sounds of the ship trying to break free. Everyone was on edge. We carried on with our regular onboard activities.

The dining room and the lounge stayed open, keeping their regular hours. Having the piano music that I played in the lounge helped me and everyone else relax and brought a calm to us all.

Pictured below: Canadian Ice Breaker on its way to save us.
Pictures courtesy of the author

Three long days later, relief arrived when we saw the Canadian icebreaker and saw that it was slowly coming towards us. It maneuvered through the ice to reach us, which took another two days. Its hulking presence was both very comforting and surreal. We didn't know if it would be successful in breaking open a path to free us.

The ship got close enough to refuel us and then slowly cut its way through the ice and maneuvered its way in front of us to open a path for us. It was a tremendous relief when we finally knew that the icebreaker had been successful. We had been freed from the ice, and we were underway again.

I looked for my friends, the Russian couple, but they were gone. I realized that they had quietly disembarked and boarded the icebreaker. I never saw them again.

After we got underway again, we learned that our final destination had changed. Instead of Dutch Harbor, Alaska, we were now heading to Nova Scotia, Canada. I didn't care where we ended up—I just wanted to get home safely.

I learned that before reaching Nova Scotia, we would make one last stop at Ellesmere Island, home to an Inuit village named Griese Fiord, located just 900 miles from the North Pole. As the ship prepared for the final excursion, the captain appeared in the lounge again. I had hoped that I wouldn't see him again. I hoped that he'd be too busy saving us to have time to go to the lounge.

When he came in, he looked at me. His look let me know that he hadn't forgotten about me. I knew that he was still a threat to me.

The next day, I went to see the ship's doctor in his small office. He gestured for me to sit across from him, his expression calm but curious as he leaned forward slightly. "What brings you here?" he asked, his voice low and measured.

Taking a deep breath, I explained everything—the captain's unsettling words, the heavy sense of dread that lingered in my cabin each night, and my fear that he might act on his threats. The doctor's demeanor changed instantly. His eyes narrowed, not in doubt, but in quiet understanding. He didn't question a single detail. He was someone who knew the captain.

After a pause, he nodded. "I have a friend," he said, his voice steady. "He's a bush pilot and will be on Ellesmere Island tomorrow, at the Inuit village of Grise Fiord. I can arrange for him to fly you to safety."

He outlined the plan in meticulous detail: the bush pilot would take me from Ellesmere Island to Resolute Bay, then I would fly back to Edmonton, and finally, to Seattle. But it wouldn't be simple. "You'll have to leave the ship in secret," he warned. "Once you go, there's no turning back."

The weight of his words settled over me. The alternative—spending more days at sea until we reached Nova Scotia, under the captain's shadow—was a risk that I couldn't take. I looked at him and nodded firmly. "I'll go."

"Good," he said, his tone sharp and decisive. "Pack everything you brought with you and wait for my call tomorrow morning. After the call, go to the purser's office—they'll give you cash for your flights. Board the zodiac with the others, but don't let on that anything is amiss."

The pilot will find you on the island and guide you. You'll stay behind while the others return to the ship."

I swallowed hard and whispered, "I understand."

The next morning, I was ready. My backpack was packed tightly, containing every belonging I'd brought on this ill-fated expedition. The phone rang, and the doctor's voice was steady as he said, "All of the arrangements have been made. Good luck and safe travels." I thanked him, slinging my backpack over my shoulder and heading out. My heart pounded as I walked to the purser's office. The clerk handed me an envelope containing $700 in cash. I slipped it into my wallet, zipped my backpack closed, and moved on to the zodiac loading area, keeping my expression neutral.

The ride to Ellesmere Island was no different than the others—icy wind biting my face, the roar of the engine, and the rhythmic bouncing of the raft over the frigid sea. Onshore, a group of Inuit villagers waited to greet us, their presence instantly bringing to life the childhood memories I had of visiting the Eskimo exhibit at the Museum of Natural History.

There were about seventy-five Inuit people in Grise Fiord, spanning generations from babies bundled against the cold to elders who moved with timeless grace. Small houses dotted the landscape, their exteriors battered by relentless Arctic winds. In the distance, a two-story metal building stood as the village's centerpiece. The scent of drying animal skins hung in the air, stretched over driftwood racks, while men in canoes skillfully navigated the icy waters, hunting seals and whales.

Women with thick black braids tended to their children, their hands swift and purposeful.

Others zipped past on snowmobiles provided by the Canadian government, modern machinery juxtaposed against a way of life that had endured for thousands of years.

I moved among the passengers, careful to act like this was just another excursion. Inside, my nerves churned as I scanned the shore, waiting for the bush pilot who would lead me away from this frozen edge of the world.

In Picture: Inuit Eskimos at Gris Fiord, Ellesmere Island, courtesy of the author

In Picture: bush pilot on Ellesmere Island who would fly me to safety, courtesy of the author

Making my Escape...
with the Bush Pilot

I saw the bush pilot standing by his small twin-engine plane. He glanced in my direction, giving me a look that said he knew who I was. Without a word or gesture to hint at our secret plan, he kept his distance, waiting for the right moment to approach me. I stayed close to the group, acting as if nothing unusual was happening, but my heart raced in anticipation.

There was a small store in the village, the Gris Fiord Co-op. It was stocked with essential supplies like food, toiletries, and laundry soap, along with remarkable Inuit artwork. Sculptures carved from tusks and what appeared to be green, glass-like stone caught my eye. They were sculptures of whales, birds, and polar bears. Some of them were engraved with drawings with what looked like black ink. Each one was a testament to the Inuit's artistry and deep connection to their environment. The pieces were breathtakingly beautiful—and expensive.

Some passengers purchased them as souvenirs, but I could only admire their craftsmanship.

We were invited into a gymnasium inside the two-story metal building for a welcoming ceremony. The Inuit villagers, dressed in ceremonial clothing made from animal skins and adorned with intricate feathered headdresses, performed for us. Their drums and shakers, handmade from animal skins, resonated deeply as they sang and danced. It felt like stepping into a living history, a glimpse into traditions passed down through countless generations. The performance was mesmerizing, their music and movements telling stories of resilience and survival in this frozen wilderness.

Our visit was brief—daylight was short, and we needed to leave before the ice became too treacherous. After the ceremony, the group headed outside to board the zodiac. As they filed towards the raft, the bush pilot appeared beside me and motioned subtly for me to follow him. My pulse quickened. This was it.

He led me to an upstairs room in the metal building. The room was sparsely furnished with a couch and a small table, but it felt warm compared to the biting cold outside. The temperature was ten below zero and would be dropping. The pilot, rugged and older, exuded a calm confidence in his heavy work clothes and baseball cap.

"Sit down," he said, his voice steady. Despite the circumstances, I did not feel threatened by him or scared of him. He was a friend of the doctor who had agreed to aide me in my escape. He handed me a form to sign—a document I didn't bother to read. My focus was on leaving, not on paperwork. As soon as I signed it, he explained that we'd wait until the ship set sail before heading to his plane.

From the window, I watched the group boarding the zodiac. A man on the shore noticed my absence and started pacing around and throwing his arms up in the air. He seemed agitated, but eventually, he climbed into the zodiac. The zodiac pushed off, and I watched as it returned to the ship. After it returned to the ship, the ship's horn blared a farewell as it left the island—without me.

"Time to go," the pilot said, motioning for me to follow.

The temperature outside was steadily dropping. As we approached the plane, he climbed in and attempted to start the engines. Nothing. Again, he tried. Still nothing.

"They're frozen," he said matter-of-factly. I knew that I had to leave. I couldn't stay behind in the Eskimo village. "Is there anything that I can do?" I asked pleadingly.

He retrieved a small contraption from the plane, a box with a T-shaped handle, and explained that I could use it to pump warm air into the engines. He attached cables to the engines and handed me the handle. "Just pump this up and down," he instructed. Then, to my astonishment, he went back inside the building, leaving me alone in the ten-below-zero Arctic cold.

Bundled in my red parka, my giant blue mittens, and my men's insulated boots, I began pumping furiously. The freezing air bit at my face, and my arms ached from the repetitive motion, but I kept going. After what felt like an eternity, the pilot returned, unhooked the cables, and climbed back into the cockpit.

The engines sputtered a few times as my life flashed before me. After several tries, the engine turned over. Relief flooded through me. The pilot helped me climb onto the wing, and I got into the passenger seat. He got in on the other side, took his place at the controls, and moments later, we were airborne.

Almost immediately, I felt nauseous. "I think I'm going to be sick," I confessed.

He handed me a paper bag and glanced over with a faint smile. "Don't worry, I'm going to take you to safety. You're on your way home!" he said, trying to lighten the mood.

To distract me, he offered to let me "help steer" the plane. I placed my hands on the secondary steering wheel in front of me, trying not to actually move it. I suspected later that they weren't actually connected, but the simple act of having something to do to helped calm my nerves. As we flew over breathtaking fjords and untouched Arctic landscapes, he pointed out features below. "No human has ever walked where you are seeing," he said, his voice filled with awe. "Get your camera out!" he said.

I reached into my backpack, forgetting about the steering wheel for a minute, seeing that he had the situation under control. The beauty of the scene helped me relax. I managed to take a few photos, capturing the otherworldly splendor of the Arctic from above. The pilot's kindness and composure reassured me. My breathing became more relaxed, and I knew that I would make it back safely.

We landed in Resolute just in time for me to catch the only flight leaving that day to Edmonton. Before parting, the pilot handed me a bottle of water and wished me well. I thanked him sincerely, knowing how lucky I was to have had his help.

Inside the small airport, I purchased a ticket with the $700 cash the purser had given me. It was just enough to get to Edmonton and then back home to Seattle. During the flight to Edmonton, the airline handed out certificates commemorating our journey above the Arctic Circle. I stuffed mine into my bag, but it was lost somewhere along the way. No matter—I wasn't about to go back to get another one.

When I finally arrived in Seattle, Rich was waiting to pick me up. Exhausted and thinner than when I'd left, I collapsed into his spare bedroom, grateful to be home.

My Arctic adventure was over, and though the memories would stay with me forever, I started to dream of moving forward, leaving the icy wilderness behind for good.

In Picture: The SS World Discoverer (picture: public domain)

The MS World Discoverer now lays abandoned off the coast of Somalia, with no one claiming ownership to it. I believe that my cabin is the part that jets out and sits in front of the racks that once held its life boats.

Working on the Road... and... onboard a Cruise Ship to Alaska!

I took time to recover and to make notes about my Arctic journey. Though I still had my apartment in the University District with my roommates, Natalie and Shelley, I felt no desire to return to it—or to the Arts college. It was August, and I wanted to move forward. Rich, busy with nightclub gigs until the early hours, encouraged me to rest and plan my next steps while staying in his spare bedroom.

One evening, as we talked about the future, the idea of forming a duo act and working on the road together began to take shape. Rich decided to take a year off from finishing his classical guitar performance degree, and I was resolved never to set foot in the Arts college again. The decision was made—neither of us was returning to school that fall. We were excited and dived headfirst into creating something new.

Weeks were spent rehearsing, crafting set lists, and assembling our promo package. Rich's connections with a booking agency smoothed the process. Together, we selected songs in diverse genres—R&B, rock, country, Top 40—tailored to the variety of venues we'd play. I immersed myself in learning how to program drum tracks and horn lines for our background tracks, fine-tuning every detail. We worked tirelessly to perfect our sound, often losing track of time during late-night rehearsals.

We named our act Take Two. With glossy 8x10 headshots and a polished demo tape, we presented ourselves as a duo that sounded like a full band: bass, drums, keyboard, guitar, and two vocalists with horn lines layered in. My keyboard featured a "split key" function—notes below the split played bass lines, while notes above handled piano chords and melodies. I also sang, taking on the roles of bass player, keyboardist, and main vocalist. Rich played guitar and sang harmonies, occasionally taking the lead. After a few more meetings with Rich's agent, we were ready to hit the road.

We were booked as a variety act, prepared to perform everything from rock to country, and we stayed current with pop tunes. Whether it was a dance hall, a smoky bar, or a polished lounge, we were ready to adapt. We were a dance band as well, tailoring our sets to fit whatever room we walked into.

We packed Rich's van with our gear and began touring a circuit arranged by the agency, covering Idaho, Montana, Utah, Oregon, and eventually circling back to Seattle. Life on the road was grueling but exhilarating. Each night brought a new crowd, teaching me to read the room and adapt to diverse audiences. Rich, a seasoned performer, was my mentor in navigating the nuances of playing various styles, and he helped me refine my sequencing skills. Over the next seven years, we worked the Northwest circuit, gaining experience and building our reputation.

One room in particular stood out to me, not for its glamour but for its rough-and-tumble atmosphere. The club was in a tiny town with a tough crowd. As we set up, we noticed 4-foot-tall chicken wire stretched across the front of the stage. We both realized that it was there to protect the band from flying objects if the audience didn't like the music.

I had brought along a sleek black tuxedo outfit that I loved—a waist-high, long-sleeved jacket, slim-fitted pants, and black heels. It was hip, classy, and my usual go-to for gigs. But after seeing the chicken wire and getting a feel for the room, I decided to not to change and played the night in my jeans.

Fortunately, Rich read the room perfectly, picking just the right tunes to win over the rowdy crowd. We started with "Old Time Rock and Roll," a classic rock tune. By the end of the night, they were drunk, laughing, and singing along. The scene felt like something straight out of The Blues Brothers movie—chaotic, loud, and brimming with wild energy. The chicken wire turned out to be unnecessary, but I was a little glad it was there... just in case. In a room like that, with a crowd like that, you never knew what might happen.

Another memorable night in a different small town took an unexpected turn. The venue was what we'd call "a dive," but the dance floor was packed with people having a great time. Out of nowhere, I heard the sharp sound of glass breaking. I glanced over and saw one guy hitting another guy over the head with a bottle. A fight broke out, fists flying, and the scene turned chaotic.

Strangely enough, most of the dancers just kept dancing, unfazed by the commotion around them.

Rich and I looked at each other briefly, me wondering if we should stop playing—but we didn't. We just kept going, the music acting like a buffer against the chaos. Even when the police arrived, hauling a few people out, the rest of the crowd never missed a beat. The band keeps going, no matter what...they even kept playing on the Titanic.

I was glad to get out of there. We just never knew what kind of room that we'd get booked into. Sometimes, the agent would get it wrong. We'd be told it was a Top 40 room - and it'd turn out to be hard-core Country. I learned a lot in those seven years, and when a new opportunity came along, I had some reservations, but I was ready to get off of the circuit.

Headshot of the author taken in 1986
"Take Two Duo" courtesy of Lynn DeBonn

We were on a break from the circuit when our agent called. He had something different—a job on a cruise ship. The ship would travel from Vancouver, Canada, along the Inside Passage to Alaska and back. ...that sounded familiar. ..a cruise ship job going to Alaska. The trip was three weeks long. Memories of the Arctic expedition still haunted me, and the thought of returning to a ship filled me with apprehension. But Rich, ever persuasive, assured me that it wouldnt be anything like my previous experience. "This is a CRUISE ship, not an EXPEDITION," he stressed, "and you won't be by yourself," he reminded me.

Reluctantly, I agreed. We drove to Vancouver, parked the van, and boarded the cruise ship. The scale of the vessel dwarfed the World Explorer—it carried over 3,000 passengers and 500 crew members. As we settled into our passenger cabins, I allowed myself to feel cautiously optimistic. We didn't have to lug around heavy gear; the ship provided a fully equipped stage with a PA system and keyboard. It seemed like a good start.

That illusion faded quickly. Shortly after boarding, we met the band director, who was a professional-looking guy in his thirties from New York who talked fast and had a full head of black wavy hair. "Nice to meet you, Maureen and Rich. I'll show you the room where you'll be playing tomorrow after you go to the muster meeting at 8:00 a.m. in the crew lounge." ...crew lounge? muster meeting? .." You and Rich will have some "crew duties" in addition to your performances." Hearing the words "crew duties" brought a faint feeling of dread. I asked, "do we HAVE to go?" He answered, "Yes, you HAVE to go to the muster meeting, but it's no big deal... just information that you have to be given because you and Rich are also crew members." I didn't want to go. I groaned inwardly, recalling my earlier experience on board the expedition. Still, there was no turning back now.

We went to the muster meeting the following morning at 8:00 a.m. I hadn't even had any coffee and felt groggy and annoyed about attending the "muster meeting," whatever that was. The room buzzed with casually chatting crew members sitting at tables. An officer from the ship began the meeting. He said, "good morning, everyone. Tomorrow morning at 8:00 a.m., British officers will arrive to inspect the ship." He explained the inspection would include a mock drill outlining the scenario. "When the alarm sounds, all crew members (which now included me and Rich) will report to the ships lounge. You will line up in front of the stage, and one person will be chosen to demonstrate how to respond in an emergency. That crew member will put on their life jacket, help passengers into theirs, and instruct them to line up single file, holding the waist of the person in front of them. Then, they will lead the passengers to the lifeboats."

He demonstrated how to put on a life jacket, told us that there would be life jackets located on tables in the lounge, and then we were dismissed. I didn't think that I was paying close attention or that there could be any way that the crew member chosen to do this could possibly be ME. After all, Rich and I had just gotten on board the ship. Everyone else had already been on board for a few weeks.

I found the band director after the meeting and said, "there's NO WAY that I could possibly selected......right?" He grinned. "No way, don't worry about it." He went on to tell me that there was very little chance that I could be selected... "a one in 500 chance." His words were comforting, but he offered a final piece of advice: "Look, when the officers get to you, make sure to look them straight in the eyes. They're looking for the guy who's staring at his shoes - not someone who looks confident."

The next morning at 8:00 a.m., the alarm blared. Sleepy and without having any coffee, I joined the other 498 crew members in the ship's lounge. We lined up single file across the room, our backs to the stage. I stood somewhere in the middle of the line with Rich next to me on my right.

The British officers, dressed in crisp white uniforms with gleaming black shoes, began inspecting from the far left. They stopped in front of each crew member, scrutinizing them briefly before moving on. I silently willed them to pick someone else each time they paused.

Slowly, they inched closer.

They got to Rich, looked him over, and then went on to me. I remembered the band director's advice and looked the lead officer directly in the eyes. He locked eyes with me, pointed, and bellowed, "YOU!"

He stepped forward and screamed: "THE SHIP'S ON FIRE! GET THE PASSENGERS TO THE LIFEBOATS!" Then, louder, he repeated, "THE SHIP'S ON FIRE! EVACUATE THE PASSENGERS!"

Holy cow. They chose ME!

Something snapped into place. Without thinking, I leapt into action like an alter ego had taken over. I grabbed a life jacket, secured it with a snap, and went over to passengers standing in a group across the room. I yelled at them: "Everyone, grab a life jacket and put it on!" My voice carried authority, and people scrambled to follow my instructions. I checked quickly to make sure that they all had their jackets on.

"Now, form a single-file line! Hold on to the waist of the person in front of you!" I barked, moving to the front of the line. Follow me!" ..and they all did. With the passengers in tow, I lead the line through the hallways to the lifeboats. We reached the deck, where the lifeboats hung, ready to deploy. Had it been a real emergency, we would have boarded them. My demonstration had gone off without a hitch.

There were a few other mock drills that were done that day in a different parts of the ship, but none as big and dramatic or as important as ours. In the other drills, crew members had to demonstrate that they knew how to respond to different types of fires and which type of fire extinguisher to use for the type of fire they were putting out. They had to answer questions, but they didn't have to re-enact a scenario that they were given to save the passengers.

Later that day, the captain summoned me to his office. His expression was a mix of gratitude and pride. "Your performance earned us a five-star rating," he said. "If we hadn't passed that drill, the ship would've been docked, and passengers would have been sent home. That would've been disastrous for everyone."

I waited, half-expecting a bonus, but his thanks were all I received. Oh well... I started counting the days.

Meanwhile, onshore, passengers from the ship recognized me in a small town we'd stopped at, pointing and whispering. For the day, I was a minor celebrity, though I felt more like I'd survived an audition for some high-stakes reality show.

That evening, I ran into the band director. I didn't say anything at first, but he grinned knowingly. After a pause, I tilted my head, looking HIM straight in the eyes, and said, "Thanks for the advice" ... we all had a good laugh... and raised a toast with several cocktails.

That night, after we went to bed, I felt relieved that our "mock drill" was over.

The next morning, a large Russian cleaning woman knocked on my cabin door. I thanked her for coming and told her that I she didn't need to do any cleaning for me. She didn't seem to understand English well. To express my gratitude and to get her to leave, I gifted her a pair of alligator pumps that were too big for me. Her reaction was unexpected. Overwhelmed with joy, she picked me up, threw me over her shoulder, and carried me down the hallway and down a flight of stairs to the crew deck.

I didn't want to make a scene, so I kept asking her in a quiet voice, "please put me down!" Next thing I knew, she was parading me through a row of bunk beds draped with makeshift curtains, eventually depositing me in a common area filled with long tables and a spinning disco ball. The crew members were partying wildly, their laughter and music echoing through the space. I made a quick exit at the first opportunity and found my way back to our cabin. I was starting to see that there was a hierarchy that existed onboard the ship and that, once again, playing on board a ship was already tuning into another odyssey.

Rich and I enjoyed passenger-level privileges—spacious cabins, access to buffets, and freedom to join day trips. Below us, on the crew deck, lived the Filipino band we alternated sets with and the other crew members who were service staff. They were confined to eating in the mess hall and shared bunk-style accommodations. On the lowest deck, the engine room level were workers from Pakistan. Their existence was hidden from passengers. We only glimpsed them once, sitting cross-legged near a metal door, smoking cigarettes. Their gaunt figures left a lasting impression. They were never allowed to be seen by the passengers.

Life on the ship felt surreal, a floating microcosm where we performed nightly, mingled with passengers and explored remote port towns.

Our first stop was Ketchikan, a small, picturesque town that greeted us with a biting chill. The water shimmered a deep, glassy blue, framed by distant snow-capped mountains. We found a cozy coffee shop nestled along the waterfront, its windows fogged from the warmth inside. With lattes in hand, we sank into our seats, savoring the steam curling from our cups. The scene outside was like a postcard—nature's majesty reflected in the pristine waters, flanked by rugged peaks. It was both serene and humbling.

Afterward, we ventured out to explore. Quaint shops lined the streets, their wooden signs creaking slightly in the cold breeze. We strolled past displays of carved totems and fishing gear, the crisp air nipping at our faces. Despite the town's charm, the cold seeped into our bones, and soon, we retreated to the warmth of the ship, content with our brief but enchanting visit.

A few days later, our next stop was a place called Whittier, a remote settlement nestled in the wilderness. The town was accessible only by train, cruise ships that docked there, or a one- lane tunnel cutting through the mountains to a larger town. It was already getting dark and freezing cold as we disembarked with other passengers. Together, we made our way down a narrow plank set up to reach the shore, crossing a set of railroad tracks and following the only road in town.

At the end of the road stood a small bar, where a lone musician played keyboard and sang through a PA system. His performance was impressive, almost surreal, given the isolated setting. It felt like we could have been in any small-town bar in America, but instead, we were in one of the most isolated places imaginable. The strangeness of it all was palpable.

Crew members who had been here before joked about the locals, affectionately—or perhaps not so affectionately—calling them

"Whidiots." The nickname seemed to stem from the peculiar way life was organized there. The entire population of about 200 people lived in a single, towering thirteen-story former army barracks at one end of the town. Everything they needed—grocery store, post office, school, police station—was contained within that one building. The only other notable structure in town was the bar at the opposite end of the lone road.

The oddity of Whittier left an impression. It was both charming and unsettling to see an entire community condensed into such a small, self-contained world. After enjoying the warmth of the bar and the lively music, we made our way back to the ship. Whittier was an unforgettable stop on our journey, but I was glad to leave its peculiar atmosphere behind as we sailed on to our next destination.

Our next stop was Juneau, the capital of Alaska. Nestled between towering, snow-draped mountains and bordered by deep blue waters, the town exuded a rugged, understated charm. I had read that it was famous for its wildlife and a favorite destination for cruise ship passengers seeking adventure and natural beauty.

We arrived the next morning under a crisp, clear sky. The air was icy, carrying the unmistakable freshness of the Alaskan wilderness. Small, colorful houses dotted the landscape, their bright hues standing in cheerful contrast against the wintry backdrop. The town seemed to hug the base of the mountains as if seeking shelter from the vastness beyond.

We set out for a walk along a quiet sidewalk that wound past modest one-story homes and a hotel that rose a few stories higher, its weathered façade hinting at years of enduring the elements. The streets were quiet, with only a few people milling about. The stillness made the grandeur of the surrounding wilderness even more striking. Towering evergreens climbed the slopes, and wisps of mist hung in the distance, adding a touch of mystery to the scene.

As we strolled, I found myself captivated by the unspoiled beauty of the place. The simplicity of the town seemed to blend seamlessly with the dramatic landscape, as if life here was designed to exist in harmony with nature. The cold air nipped at our faces and hands, but the views made it worth braving the chill. Every glance reminded me that we were in a part of the world that remained largely untouched by the chaos of modern life.

I had read about the whales that sometimes passed by, their majestic presence a highlight for visitors. While we didn't spot any that day, the thought of them swimming in the icy waters just beyond our view added a sense of wonder to the experience. The only "wildlife" we encountered that day were a few of the locals, bundled against the cold, some with a drink in hand, even in the early hours. Life here seemed slow-paced. There was a quiet resilience to the people and the town itself.

After exploring the small blocks and soaking in the tranquil atmosphere, we decided to head back to the ship. The serene simplicity and the majesty of Juneau and its surroundings left an impression of the beauty to be found in the capitol of Alaska.

Our next stop was Anchorage. As we disembarked, we learned about a walking tour that was just about to begin. Curious, we joined a group of passengers and began climbing a hill in the center of town. At the top, we arrived at a cluster of old, weather-beaten shacks—grim remnants of the gold rush era. The shacks had housed women who lived and worked as prostitutes, providing services to miners who sought companionship in the harsh, unforgiving conditions of the frontier in the 1890's.

Inside the shacks, the stark reality of their lives was laid bare. The rooms were damp and dark with few windows, worn-out wooden floors, rusted metal bed frames, and a few other sparse items. The mattresses were faded and dirty, some torn open to reveal sagging springs. Dark, oil- soaked rags were draped at the ends of the beds—makeshift barriers to keep the miners' muddy boots from soiling what little comfort the women had. A single dim lantern hung from the ceiling in one shack, casting shadows over the cracked wooden walls.

On old, worn wooden tables were displays of photographs and artifacts. The pictures of the women—some posed in shifts and tattered dresses—revealed stories of endurance etched onto their faces. Hard lines and weary eyes spoke of lives marked by struggle and survival. Many of the women wore old dresses with laced-up boots, their smiles faint or absent altogether.

Alongside these images were photos of some of their clients: rough, unkempt men with missing teeth and weathered faces, the kind who seemed more at home in the wild than among civilization. I tried to imagine the world these women had inhabited—a world where every day was a fight to survive, where their work was both a necessity and a source of judgment.

Seeing their lives displayed this way felt invasive, as if their stories were being retold without their consent.

Some artifacts added to the heavy atmosphere. A faded journal, written in shaky handwriting, sat open to a page describing a night's earnings. Empty bottles of whiskey hinted at the ways these women coped with their realities. Heavy, scuffed boots lined the floor near the beds, left behind as if their owners had stepped out and never returned.

While some on the tour seemed fascinated by the history, I couldn't shake the unease I felt. These women had lived hard lives, exploited for the comfort of others, and now, even in death, their existence had been turned into a tourist attraction. It felt wrong. These shacks, once a place of desperation and resilience, were now part of a macabre spectacle for curious visitors.

I only went into one shack. That was enough for me. Outside, the air felt cold and heavy, matching the weight in my heart. I wished these women could have been left to keep their secrets, their hardships allowed to fade into the past rather than be immortalized as an object of curiosity. They had endured enough during their lives; they deserved to rest in peace.

After the tour, we walked back down the hill. We stopped briefly at a small local shop to browse, but my thoughts remained with the women and the lives they had led. Returning to the ship, I felt a somber sense of gratitude for the freedoms I had but also a deep sadness for the sacrifices of those who had come before. The breathtaking scenery of the journey had often left me in awe, but this stop in Anchorage left me reflecting on the human cost of history—and the ways we choose to remember it.

We returned to the ship, my mind still heavy with the somber history of the tour. Stepping onto the stage that evening, I felt a sense of relief as the beauty of the music enveloped me. As we played, the weight of the day began to lift, replaced by the joy of sharing music with others. Watching the passengers smile, tap their feet, and sway to the melodies reminded me of the transformative power of music—a universal language that could momentarily erase sorrow and replace it with connection and happiness.

Our final destination was Glacier Bay, an experience that became the undeniable highlight of the journey. As the ship glided through the frigid, steel-blue waters, the glaciers came into view, their immense walls of ice shimmering with an otherworldly bluish tint. The sunlight caught their jagged edges, creating a mesmerizing interplay of light and shadow that made the scene feel almost surreal.

We stood on the deck, bundled against the biting cold, captivated by the sight. Towering above us, the glaciers seemed to breathe with a slow, unrelenting power. The stillness of the moment was interrupted only by the dramatic phenomenon of calving—when massive chunks of ice broke away from the glacier's face. The sound was unforgettable: deep, resonant groans echoed like distant thunder, followed by sharp cracks and a deafening splash as the ice plunged into the sea below. Ripples radiated outward, rocking the surrounding ice floes as though the bay itself was alive and reacting to the spectacle.

It felt like we were witnessing a performance staged by nature herself—raw, primal, and utterly awe-inspiring. I couldn't help but marvel at the glaciers' dual nature: ancient and unyielding, yet constantly in flux, shaped by forces beyond human control. This living museum of ice and history was a reminder of the Earth's enduring cycles of creation and destruction, beauty and peril.

As the ship slowly made its way around Glacier Bay, I lingered on the deck, reluctant to leave this magnificent place behind. The icy expanse, with its towering glaciers and the eerie symphony of cracking and splashing ice, felt like a sacred space—untouched, untamed, and profoundly humbling.

After we left Glacier Bay, we began our return to Vancouver, British Columbia, the final leg of our journey. Relief swept over me as we docked, and I stepped off the ship for the last time. I was ready to leave this floating world behind and return to something solid, something familiar.

Driving back to Seattle with Rich, I felt a mixture of exhaustion and clarity. Seven years as a professional musician had taught me resilience, adaptability, and the nuances of working with people and audiences. But it also left me yearning for something more—something that aligned better with who I was becoming as an artist.

The cruise had affirmed one thing: life on a ship wasn't for me. The rigid hierarchy onboard, the seasickness that hit at the worst moments, and the endless buffets that lost their appeal after the first few days—it wasn't a life I wanted to pursue. While I appreciated the beauty of the places we visited and the chance to connect with audiences, I was ready for a new chapter.

Back in Seattle, I felt a renewed determination to find opportunities that would allow me to grow, to challenge myself, and to create music that resonated on a deeper level. The cruise was a chapter I was glad to close, knowing it had played its part in shaping my path forward. The road ahead was uncertain, but for the first time in a long while, it felt like I was truly ready to move forward.

Working on my Own

I decided to put my own act together as a soloist, book myself, and give piano bars a try. I landed a weekend gig playing in a lounge, and it turned out to be a great success, lasting for five years.

When I first started, the lounge would be nearly empty, while the dining room next to it was packed. The diners could hear my piano music but couldn't see me. After dinner, many of them would wander into the lounge for cocktails and stay to enjoy the music. During the dinner hour, I only played piano over my bass and drum tracks, saving my singing for later in the evening. Several times, patrons approached me, surprised to find out I was a woman. "I thought you were a guy," they'd say. Maybe it was the confidence in my playing that led them to assume that—I took it as a compliment.

Everything changed once I started singing. While they enjoyed the piano music, they fell in love with my voice. I have a bluesy style that brought a fresh feel to the pop songs I sang, and I threw in some blues numbers, too. Singing and accompanying myself on piano felt natural, and over time, I developed a loyal following of fans who became "regulars." By Friday night, they'd already be in the lounge, waiting for me to arrive. Many stayed until closing time, week after week.

Walking into the lounge each Friday night felt like stepping into a Norman Rockwell painting. The same faces, the same seats—it was as if nothing ever changed. At that time, smoking was still allowed in bars, and the piano bar was designed with a built-in table around the piano where guests could sit, drink, and chat. It meant I often had people close to me while I performed who were smoking and drinking while I was playing and singing. The more they drank, the more they smoked. Some people would even have more than one cigarette going at a time— one smoldering in the ashtray while they puffed on another or using the current one to light the next.

I liked to tell jokes between songs to the folks gathered around the piano. One night, a lady sat right in front of me, smoking like a chimney. She was pretty drunk, and every time she exhaled, a cloud of hazy, stinky cigarette smoke drifted straight into my face. It wasn't intentional—she was just too drunk to notice.

She leaned in close, clutching her cigarette in one hand and her drink in the other, her voice slow and slurred. "Honey... you don't mind if I smoke while you're singing, do you?" I smiled politely and replied, "Hey, it's fine... just don't exhale, OK?"

She and the rest of the group thought that was hilarious... They were all pretty drunk, laughing and coughing in the smoke-filled haze.

The cigarette smoke really started to take a toll on me after a couple of years, even though I only played on the weekends. One night, on my way home, the nausea hit so hard that I had to pull off the road at two a.m., get out of my car, and throw up. That was the moment I realized I needed to find another way to make a living with my music. I couldn't keep playing in nightclubs, lounges, or piano bars—it was suffocating me, literally and figuratively.

I knew I had to stay in music. My years of experience and education were too valuable to waste. I needed to create something new for myself, to move forward and leave the lounge scene behind. I didn't want to play in another smoky piano bar, another nightclub, or on another ship. There had to be another path out there for me.

Just as I was reaching this crossroads, a friend who often came out to hear me play asked me, "Have you ever heard of the Washington State Music Teachers Association?"

Her suggestion changed my life.

Finding Meaning – and a
New Way Forward

I reached out to the local chapter of the Washington State Music Teachers Association (WSMTA) and was invited to one of their meetings. It was a gathering of local piano teachers who met monthly at a member's home. They welcomed me warmly, excited to have me join as a new member. At the time, I didn't have much teaching experience beyond working as a student teacher for a jazz pianist during my time at the Arts College. But, the WSMTA provided me with the education and resources I needed to thrive as a piano teacher and learn how to successfully run my own piano studio.

I had an intuitive way of connecting with students, tailoring my approach to their individual learning styles and interests while making the process of learning the piano enjoyable. My classical training, combined with my ability to play in any style, allowed me to offer a unique and engaging experience. Sometimes, I'd show students how to sprinkle in a few blues licks or experiment with different genres, and they'd light up, eager to learn more. We had so much fun exploring music together, even as I taught them the fundamentals—scales, chords, and the harmonic system. I approached music much like a language: chords were the words, and the harmonic system was the grammar that tied it all together.

The WSMTA not only honed my teaching skills but also taught me the business of running a professional piano studio. While my business degree provided a foundation, the WSMTA offered invaluable insights specific to the music education field. They shared examples of studio policies, a critical tool for running a professional studio. I studied these samples and developed my own policy, carefully tailoring it to create the studio I envisioned. The WSMTA encouraged us to adapt and innovate, empowering us to build the piano studios of our dreams—a place where teaching and learning could flourish in harmony.

Soon, I had the beginnings of a thriving piano studio! I fell in love with the idea of creating a stable business for myself, doing exactly what I loved and was trained to do. What surprised me most was how much I fell in love with teaching—and with my students. They, in turn, fell in love with me too. It doesn't get better than that.

My extensive performing experience and ability to play in different styles set me apart from other teachers. Many of them didn't have the same practical, real-world experience. For me and my students, this was invaluable—it brought a unique energy to my lessons, making teaching both rewarding and fun.

I built a professional business that I could depend on to make a living, something I don't think I could have achieved without the knowledge and support I gained from the WSMTA. Their guidance laid the foundation for my success.

The WSMTA meetings were a treasure trove of inspiration and learning. Each meeting often featured a special guest—pianists from our state universities and colleges—who would perform, give lectures, and share demonstrations. They taught us about piano technique, the styles and time periods of the great composers, and how to interpret these works with historical and artistic accuracy. Their insights went beyond music, weaving connections to the art and architecture of the eras that shaped the composers' creations.

We also delved into the fascinating history of the piano itself. Today's "modern" piano has a legacy spanning over 300 years, and our studies reached back to its earliest days.

Remarkably, some of the technical exercises and compositions from those early times remain foundational to piano education. The enduring works of the great composers, combined with centuries of tradition, continue to inspire and guide both teachers and students.

Private teachers often held their own recitals for their students, but there was also an annual opportunity for students from different studios to perform together in a recital adjudicated by a master teacher from one of the universities. These recitals not only provided valuable performance experience for the students but also included critiques for the teachers. The master pianist would sometimes offer private master classes to students, and we, as teachers, were invited to observe. It was an incredible opportunity for both students and teachers to grow and deepen their musical education.

After attending meetings for about a year, one of the teachers approached me with an unexpected opportunity. She planned to go on an extended vacation and asked if I would take over her well-established basement studio during her absence. She had about twenty students. I was thrilled at the prospect but suggested that, before she left, I observe her teaching and learn how she ran her studio. She agreed, and we spent time together preparing for the transition.

When she left, I found myself teaching a full studio one-on-one for the first time. The experience was both challenging and rewarding.

From the beginning, I focused on understanding each student's unique strengths and interests. If I sensed that a student was bored or disengaged, I'd find a new way to approach the music or introduce something they were excited about. My teaching style was natural, relaxed, and fun—because playing music should be fun, when you truly understand it.. you're never worried about making a mistake! You learn to never stop. You're trained to "keep going - no matter what!" ..and the music just flows along. If something happens that's unexpected, you just go with it until you get back on track... and sometimes something unexpected turns into something wonderful.

Doris's basement piano studio had two grand pianos side by side, which allowed for some creative teaching techniques. I'd often play something for a student to imitate, or we'd play together. Sometimes, I'd improvise accompaniment parts while they played melodies. This interactive approach inspired and encouraged the students, making the lessons more engaging and enjoyable.

I discovered that a lot of kids loved blues piano. I was able to show them how to improvise and play bluesy notes and licks.. and they loved it! I saw them change from students who were ready to quit - to students who couldn't wait to come for their lessons and learn more of this entirely different approach to teaching them.

The teacher who I was subbing for had been very judgmental of her students. Before she left for her vacation, she gave me a list of all of her students' names with comments that she wrote about each one. She sat down and went through the list with me before she left, telling me what she thought the short comings of each one of her students were and which students she felt really didn't have much talent. I was so surprised that she wanted to tell me everything that she felt was wrong with each one of her students. I listened, and after she left I copied down all of the names of her students...then waded up her comments about them and threw them away.

That was not going to be the way I approached teaching. I wanted to focus on each student's strengths and interests, building on what they loved and showing them new ways to explore and enjoy music. I made it a priority to teach them chords and how to identify them in their music so they could truly understand what they were playing—and we had fun doing it!

I quickly realized that the teacher I was subbing for had been trained in a method almost entirely focused on reading sheet music. She had passed this approach on to her students but lacked a deeper understanding of how the harmonic system works. Fundamental concepts, like using the three basic cadence chords in every key and playing them in simple chord progressions while creating simple melodies from the chord tones in the chords, were absent from her lessons.

These skills—rooted in improvisation—were foundational for early composers and pianists. Historical records show that improvisation was a natural part of their musical training and artistry. Yet, somewhere along the way, this essential skill has become less emphasized in traditional piano education. The term "improvisation" itself is often misunderstood, and it's rarely included as a core part of foundational lessons for pianists today, especially in private instruction.

The teacher I was subbing for had no interest or ability in improvising or playing music outside of what was written. However, it was clear to me that her students truly loved music and wanted to learn more. As I introduced these new concepts, they became more engaged and enthusiastic. When she returned from her vacation, all of her students told me they wanted to continue studying with me instead of going back to her.

I told the students to speak with their parents, who then contacted the teacher. To my surprise, she was supportive. She admitted that she had hoped this would happen. She told me she had seen something in me that made her believe I would be a good teacher and that she was ready to retire. It felt like she had passed the torch intentionally, and I was honored.

That's how my teaching career began—with a full studio of 25 students. I had discovered a new way forward, one that brought both meaning and immense joy to my life. Teaching came naturally to me, and I knew that it was a perfect fit.

To my surprise, I fell in love with my students... and they fell in love with me.

I don't know which of us looked forward more to seeing each other each week...them or me.

I set up a large room in my home with an old upright piano and my electric piano from my nightclub career. It was a humble beginning, but the music was always the most important thing. Over time, I purchased two grand pianos, and eventually, I acquired my most cherished piano— the piano of my dreams. A 1936 Steinway M. It was made at the Steinway factory in Queens, NY. We are two New Yorkers who belong together— forever.

Up until the time I bought my Steinway, whenever I worked on advanced music— especially classical pieces—I could only imagine the sound in my head. The pianos I had simply couldn't produce the sound that I could imagine. But when I brought home my beloved Steinway, the music that had once lived only in my head came to life, gloriously filling the room.

I remained in the WSMTA for several years, benefiting greatly from its outstanding education and mentorship in teaching. Each year, the association hosted a combined recital where all our students performed. We would hire a university professor to oversee the event.

Students were awarded first, second, and third place honors, and the adjudicator would meet with each one, providing feedback on their performance along with written suggestions for improving their musical and performance skills. They would also offer critiques to us, the teachers.

I grew accustomed to hearing praise like, "You've done a great job" and always, "Keep up the good work!" after our private time with the adjudicators—until I met Professor Mack. My student had placed second, and I felt proud of her performance. I expected the usual encouraging words.. and to "Keep up the good work!"

Instead, Professor Mack looked at me and asked, "Why didn't your student win first place?" I paused, caught off guard, and smiled. In that moment, I knew he was someone special... and indeed, he was. I didn't know what to say, but I didn't have to. He continued, "I'd like to hear you play. Would you come to my studio and play for me?"

I was stunned and thrilled. Professor Mack was an award-winning teacher from Ireland with a long waiting list of students hoping for a spot. I jumped at the opportunity. "I'd love to!" I said.

We made arrangements for me to visit his home studio. I chose Gershwin's Prelude No. 3 to play for him. Rated as a level 10 in difficulty—the highest level by WSMTA standards—it was a piece I adored. Though classified as classical, it was infused with jazzy, complex rhythms that were both exhilarating and challenging. I practiced tirelessly to prepare for my moment with Professor Mack.

The day of my visit, I arrived at his house and sat in my car for a moment before going in. I was nervous but excited. After pulling myself together, I knocked on his door.

His home studio was enchanting. A magnificent Steinway sat proudly in the room alongside a smaller studio piano. He had won the Steinway in a competition, a testament to his extraordinary talent.

The room itself was an eccentric treasure trove, filled with quirky knick-knacks and odd figurines he had collected from thrift stores. He used them as gifts for his students, a whimsical touch that added to his unique charm.

I played the Gershwin for him, instantly falling in love with his Steinway. Steinways have long been considered the piano of choice for musical expression and artistic development, and this one was no exception. I lost myself in the music, drifting into that otherworldly space where nothing else exists—only the sound. Sometimes, there are flashes of color, but mostly, it's the pure immersion in sound that engulfs you. In those moments, I lose all track of time, place, or reality itself.

When I finished, still half-lost in that musical realm, Professor Mack asked simply, "Would you like to study with me?"

Tears welled up inside me as the weight of my journey—its hardships and triumphs— washed over me. In that instant, it felt like all my dreams were coming true. My voice was barely more than a breath when I answered, "Oh... I'd love to."

I studied with Professor Mack for the next three years, never missing a single lesson. He was the head of the classical department at a university in Seattle but also taught a select group of "older" students, like me, in his home studio.

To prepare us for performances, he employed some very creative and unconventional "advanced performance techniques." For instance, he'd have me practice while wearing gloves or playing with distractions like the TV or radio on in the background. The most challenging exercise, however, was reading aloud from a simple children's book while playing my advanced classical piece from memory. At first, I could barely manage a word as I kept playing. Gradually, I improved—reading full sentences pausing between phrases, all while maintaining the flow of the music. The absolute rule was: no matter what, you could never stop playing.

These exercises, as frustrating as they were at times, sharpened my focus and deepened my connection to the music. When the time came for one of his recitals, held in his cozy, packed living room, I was ready. I sat at the piano, my heart racing, and began to play. Without the added challenges of his training techniques, the piece flowed effortlessly. The music swelled with emotion, filling the room and transporting me—to a new height and depth that I'd never experienced before. I was completely lost in the music and the emotion of it.

When I finished, the room erupted in applause. As I rose to take my bow, I caught the sound of a woman's whispered question: "Who IS she?"

The words brought a joyful smile to my heart. As I returned to my seat, I thought to myself, with quiet pride, I'm a student of Professor Mack's!

A Concert Career... with Opportunities for my Students

After studying with Professor Mack for three years, I made the decision to focus solely on performing in concerts. Teaching remained a cornerstone of my life, and my piano studio grew to 37 students per week. Alongside teaching, I embarked on a concert career, performing for audiences ranging from intimate gatherings of 150 to larger crowds of over 400 people.

The smaller audiences of 150 were for my students' recitals, which became cherished events for both the students and their families. Before each recital, I held a "practice recital" in my studio, followed by a piano party. These sessions were as much about building confidence as they were about music. The students performed for me and for each other, and then we celebrated together with fun and laughter. No adults were allowed—just me and the students.

They loved the exclusivity of those moments, and it created a camaraderie that added to their excitement for the upcoming recital.

The recitals themselves were held two days later, and I always opened them with a warm welcome and a performance of my own. Setting the tone for the recital was important to me—it showed my students that I wouldn't ask them to do anything I wasn't willing to do myself.

Besides, I loved performing. It gave me a chance to share the joy of music while inspiring my students to take the stage with confidence.

We made the recitals special events. I got dressed up, and my students followed suit—no sweatshirts or baseball caps were allowed. I taught them everything about performance etiquette, from how to walk gracefully to the piano to taking a proper bow. "Look down at each foot," I'd instruct, "then raise your head, smile at the audience, and return to your seat—no running!" By the time recital day arrived, they had rehearsed every detail, and their performances always shone.

The audience, composed of proud family members and friends, created an atmosphere of warmth and enthusiasm. Before each recital began, I would smile and encourage everyone to applaud after every piece, ensuring a celebratory and supportive tone. My opening performance always set the stage, receiving thunderous from both my students and their families and friends. This tradition made the recitals feel less formal and more like a shared celebration of effort and growth.

These recitals weren't just about playing the piano—they were transformative milestones.

Each student walked away with a sense of accomplishment, having faced the challenge of performing in front of an audience. Their families often marveled at how beautifully they played, but what stood out most was the confidence and poise that radiated from each child.

Piano lessons and recitals became life lessons. They nurtured creativity, encouraged innovation, and instilled resilience—skills essential for navigating our ever-changing world. Beyond the music, these experiences shaped young minds and fostered strong character, building confidence and imagination they would carry and continue to develop throughout their lives.

When I performed in larger concerts for audiences of 400 or more, they were glorious community events that brought people together to celebrate music. Our community newspaper, delivered to every resident's mailbox, featured my picture and news of these concerts on its cover for five years—the entire length of time I presented these concerts.

I drew inspiration from my Uncle Eddie, who produced spectacular shows in New York, Atlantic City, and later at Caesars Palace after our family moved to Las Vegas. Watching him had taught me the importance of professionalism and presentation, and I brought those lessons to my concerts.

I developed a format that gave structure and energy to the concert. A Master of Ceremonies would begin by welcoming the crowd, setting the tone for the evening. The concerts featured two 45-minute sets, with a 20-minute intermission in between. The first set opened with a "Student Showcase" performance—a highlight of the evening. For this, I selected a small group of "all-star" students to perform as an ensemble. The bar was set high, and the students knew they were expected to deliver a polished and confident performance.

I followed the Student Showcase with my own performance, which concluded the first set. After the intermission, the second set featured a world-renowned solo pianist or one with an ensemble of renowned musicians. The students were aware that they were "sharing the stage" with these esteemed professionals, and they embraced the challenge with dedication and excitement.

By setting high expectations, I discovered that my students not only met them—they often exceeded them. These performances were transformative, giving them a sense of achievement and a taste of the spotlight. Many went on to become music majors, and some even pursued professional careers in music. Watching them rise to the occasion and thrive was one of the most rewarding aspects of my career. I had discovered the profound rewards of building a career that I had not only self-made but was deeply meaningful. By following my passion for music and listening to my heart's true desire, I had created an extraordinarily fulfilling path for myself. Music had always been my guiding light, and now it was at the heart of a career that truly mattered. Teaching, I realized, is both a noble and transformative profession—one that shapes lives, inspires creativity, and leaves a lasting impact.

I eventually served as president of the local WSMTA chapter for three years and later founded a nonprofit organization called the South Whidbey Association of Jazz Educators.

Through this initiative, we produced our highly successful community concerts for five years. These concerts became a cornerstone of our mission, creating meaningful opportunities to advance music education and provide valuable performance experiences for local students. It was an immensely rich and rewarding endeavor that brought our community closer together through music.

In addition, I was honored to be given my own show at the performing arts center, The 88 Keys Piano Club, named after my piano studio, Maureen Girard's 88 Keys Piano Studio. Each month, I collaborated with a guest artist to design an engaging program. Together, we chose a topic to explore with the audience, performed dynamic duets on two pianos, and gave the guest artist the stage for a captivating solo set. These concerts blended education and performance, creating an intimate and enriching experience for all who attended.

My piano studio was a 900-square-foot building on my property that I had lovingly remodeled into a charming teaching space. It was warm and inviting, perfectly suited for lessons, and could also be transformed into a concert venue for house concerts. The studio featured a staging area for my two grand pianos: a stunning 1980 Yamaha and my cherished Steinway M. To enhance the atmosphere, I added six bistro tables, each with six chairs, creating a setting reminiscent of a cozy Greenwich Village nightclub. With dimmable lights, stage lighting, and a professional PA system for vocals, the studio became a magical space for both teaching and performance.

The studio's versatility allowed me to produce monthly house concerts, which quickly became cherished community events. These intimate gatherings brought audiences just feet away from the performers, creating a connection and experience unlike any traditional venue.

Grammy-nominated, platinum-selling pianist and composer David Lanz inaugurated the series in 2004 with a sensational performance. The concert was an enormous success, and my students caught what I affectionately called "Lanz Fever," diving enthusiastically into his published books of music.

Over the years, the house concerts showcased incredibly beautiful performances by world-class musicians, some traveling from as far as Argentina. Each concert celebrated the transformative power of music, blending extraordinary talent with the joy and camaraderie of an engaged and appreciative community. My studio became not just a place for learning but a vibrant hub of musical inspiration and connection.

In Picture: My beloved 88Keys Piano Studio, courtesy of the author

In Picture: Author having arrived at my true destination,
courtesy of the author

I have been fortunate to have the most wonderful and rewarding
musical career I could have ever imagined. All of my dreams have come
true, and now I find myself dreaming new dreams— dedicated to
supporting music education and fostering wellness for children through
the power of music.

I hope my story serves as an inspiration for others, especially young people whose hearts are set on pursuing a career in music. It's not an easy road, but if it's truly the right path for you, you'll find your way with determination and passion.

"What follows are heartfelt notes from my students, sharing their reflections on our time together—celebrating the joy of music and the art of the piano. Interwoven among these cherished memories, I've included a few inspirational quotes and reflections on music from notable figures such as Albert Einstein. Their words serve as a testament to the universal power of music and its ability to inspire creativity, connection, and wonder."

Notes from my Students and Stories Then..and Now, and Notable Quotes

"My piano Lessons with Maureen were a big part of my life, and to this day, I use that knowledge in my everyday life. Not only did my musical abilities grow, but those lessons also helped pinpoint the type of learner I am which made other areas of my life and learning an easier and more enjoyable experience. Maureen can identify HOW an individual student learns and can tailor the lessons accordingly. For me, that was incredibly effective and, as a professional musician now, essential." - Roy (Drums/Percussion/Synth/Composition)

Roy began taking lessons with me at age 10. He was among my very first group of students. From the start, I knew two things about him: first, that while he was learning piano, he was a drummer at heart, and second, that, like me, he was destined to become a professional musician. Nothing was going to stop him from achieving his dreams.

When I introduced Roy to blues piano and taught him basic blues chord progressions, his face lit up with excitement. He had struggled with his previous piano teacher and initially resisted letting me write out his lessons—it reminded him too much of that experience. So, I adapted my approach. I sketched out a simple blues chord progression for him and taught him the three foundational chords, along with blues scales and licks. That was the spark he needed— Roy "went nuts" with enthusiasm.

Roy quickly became a featured performer in my recitals. I always saved his performance for the grand finale. His improvised blues pieces, complete with flashy glissandos and a tremendous flair, captivated the audience, especially the other students. They were so amazed and inspired by him. The sheer joy in his playing was unmistakable, and it was clear he was a natural performer.

Roy stayed with me for several years, eventually joining the local school band as a percussionist. Roy's work ethic shone through as he excelled in both percussion and his blues piano studies.

Today, Roy lives just outside Nashville, playing drums in a famous country singer's band. He's also an accomplished songwriter, with several of his original pieces recorded by that same artist. His talent and hard work have brought him tremendous success. Roy now owns a beautiful home, purchased through his thriving music career. The songs he's written can be traced back to the blues progressions I once taught him.

I couldn't be more proud of Roy and the incredible path he's forged. I'll always cherish the memories of the years that we spent together as I watched him grow from that 10-year-old child into the polished professional that he is today. Bravo Roy!

~ ~ ~

"I don't think I would have become President if it were not for my school music program. - President Bill Clinton

~ ~ ~

This beautiful note from Kelsey holds a special place in my heart. I've read it many times over the years, especially when I needed a bit of inspiration myself. What Kelsey didn't realize is that it was she who inspired me.

"I just want you to know, Maureen, that you really saved my life when I was your student. You kept me on the right track and supported me through some tough stuff. When people ask me who I model myself after, I tell them My piano teacher. She knows so much about life and music and how to live that she's the person that I want to be. I want to have that much motivation for whatever it is that I love that I can conquer anything and succeed.

Thank you for being such an amazing human being and for sharing your wonderful gift with your students. You changed me and made me realize to be proud of myself and who I am, even when it's sucky. Thank you, Maureen, for being such a great role model and forxx genuinely caring about your students :)

- Kelsey

~ ~ ~

This heartfelt note from Kelsey brings back many fond memories. Kelsey always had a deep love for music and the piano. At the time, I wasn't fully aware of the struggles she faced at home, but I could sense that our lessons were a sanctuary for her. As soon as she sat at the piano, she would light up, her joy overflowing as the music transported her to another place. She never wanted to leave, and I cherished our time together.

Music has been a constant in Kelsey's life, a place of comfort and solace. She continues to play when she can. Since graduating with a nursing degree, she has visited me a few times to catch up and reminisce. She's shared stories of a life that has been extraordinarily challenging, yet she has persevered with remarkable grace and dignity.

I believe that music will always be a guiding light for Kelsey. One day, when she has her own piano again, I know her heart will sing as beautifully as it did when she was my student.

"Music is the universal language of mankind." — Henry Wadsworth Longfellow

~ ~ ~

A note from Grant:... and yes... I remember.

"I don't know if you remember this, but after my first day of Jazz Band in the 6th grade, I was in <u>tears</u>. I have come so far since then and <u>YOU</u> are the reason. The hours of lessons, recitals, and "Fall Concerts" have all shaped me into the musician and person I am today, and I cannot thank you enough. I would love to share a stage with you once more!

A very heartfelt thanks, Grant

~ ~ ~

Grant was "on fire" to learn jazz, driven by his desire to feel comfortable in the band, as he mentioned in his note. He worked incredibly hard, and I gave him plenty to do! He mastered standard jazz chord progressions, learned how to improvise over them, and developed the skill of playing bass lines— in all 12 keys.

When Grant came to lessons, they often turned into marathons. We'd sit at two pianos, "trading fours," challenging each other as we played. I'd call out a new key, and he'd have to transition seamlessly without missing a beat—and he did. We played up a storm together.

Grant became the primary pianist in the jazz band and one of my "all-star" performers in the Student Showcase segment of our annual "Fall Concerts," which ran for five years. His talent and dedication were instrumental in making those events successful and memorable.

Grant went on to graduate from Dartmouth College in New Hampshire, where he continued to study music as part of the college's music program. He remains an exceptional performer and is a beloved favorite in the community whenever he returns home to play.

I'm so proud of you, Grant! Thank you for the wonderful memories, the incredible performances, and for being a part of what made our Fall Concerts such a joy to create.

~ ~ ~

"Music enhances the education of our children by helping them to make connections and broadening the depth with which they think and feel. If we are to hope for a society of culturally literate people, music must be a vital part of our children's education."

– YO-YO MA, Musician

~ ~ ~

A note from Max:

"Thank you for all that you have taught me through the wonderful lessons that I have had with you. From rudimentary scales to awesome jazz piano riffs, I am so grateful for the mentoring and guidance you provided while I developed my skill on the keys. From your teaching, I have been able to find so much joy in practicing, playing, and recording music." - Max

~ ~ ~

Max was a remarkable student and one of the best I've ever seen at taking initiative and moving forward on his own. He often went well beyond the assignments I gave him, exploring additional pieces or even choosing entirely new material to work on. His curiosity and drive to learn were truly inspiring. Most importantly, he always put in the effort and had beautiful music to show for it— his independent approach was just fine with me.

Max went on to attend Stanford University, where he has continued his music studies.

Occasionally, he has come to visit, and each time I see him, I'm amazed by how much his abilities have grown. His mastery of advanced classical repertoire is a joy to hear, and his playing is nothing short of exquisite.

I have no doubt that Max will always cherish the piano and, someday...
pass his incredible gift on to his own family. Great job, Max!

~ ~ ~

A quote attributed to Albert Einstein about music: "Life without playing
music is inconceivable for me. I live my daydreams in music. I see my life
in terms of music."

A note from Chloe, who's gone on to graduate school:

~ ~ ~

Dear Maureen,

Thank you so much for nine years of piano lessons. I have learned so
much from you about piano technique, improvisation, performance,
and much more over the years, and I am excited to continue playing
piano in the future. You have also taught me so much about confidence,
dedication, perseverance, and what it means to be a truly strong woman.
Thank you for being a wonderful teacher and friend! I look forward to
seeing you when I visit home. Love,

Chloe

~ ~ ~

My time with Chloe was an absolute joy. Watching her transform from
a beginner into an advanced musician was a source of immense pride
for me. Not only did she master beautiful classical pieces, but she also
developed the ability to improvise and play jazz—a testament to her
dedication and love for music.

One unforgettable moment stands out vividly in my memory. I entered
the performing arts center and heard music I recognized, so polished
and expressive that I thought that I was listening to a recording. To
my amazement, it was Chloe! She was playing in another room, her
performance broadcast into the main stage theater. My soul lit up with
pride and joy as I realized it was her.

I also watched Chloe's confidence grow alongside her musical abilities. She's an extraordinary young woman who will undoubtedly be a force for good in the world, sharing not only her musical gifts but also the innate kindness and strength of character she has developed.

~ ~ ~

From Cory:

The piano is the best instrument of all. It can be used to play anything. And when you have a teacher like mine, music just comes to life.

Thank you, Cory

~ ~ ~

What a sweet note from Cory. He was always such a delight to teach, and his enthusiasm was contagious. He LOVED his piano lessons, and we truly shared the joy of playing the piano together. Cory always had his own ideas about the music he enjoyed and wanted to play, and I always encouraged him to follow what he loved.

Our time together was filled with wonderful memories, including the lively "piano rehearsal/parties" at my studio. Those gatherings with all the other kids were such special moments, full of laughter, music, and camaraderie. They were truly great times!

A note from my unforgettable student, Eric.

~ ~ ~

Such fond memories of playing in your studio. I was rough around the edges (to put it lightly) when I showed up on your doorstep requiring formal training. Thank you for putting up with me all those years, I don't know where I'd be without all those sight reading exercises - and letting me play your favorite tunes. Lots of nostalgia is coming back today - jamming. Here's to our upcoming duo or trio project performance! All the best,

~ ~ ~

Eric

I have such fond memories of my time with Eric. When he first arrived at my studio, he was about 9 years old and had recently been kicked out of the band program. He'd been told he would need to wait another year to rejoin. Apparently, Eric had been telling his peers to "shut up" and "don't ever play that again!" I quickly realized that his comments weren't out of malice but because he had perfect pitch—he simply couldn't tolerate hearing anything out of tune.

At his first lesson, Eric immediately made an impression. He stopped to look at himself in the mirror, holding his mouth open with his fingers and sticking out his tongue. I couldn't help but laugh—I loved it. He was a kid, full of quirks, but also incredibly talented.

Between lessons, I often played piano while waiting for students to arrive. Whatever I happened to be playing usually piqued Eric's interest. On his first day, I was playing Gershwin's Prelude No. 3, a challenging piece rated a 9 or 10 in difficulty. He begged me to teach it to him. I explained that it wouldn't be easy and told him he'd need to do two things: first, figure out a fingering that worked for his smaller hands, as the piece required a wide span, and second, keep up with his regular assignments alongside learning it.

Eric was thrilled with the arrangement. Sure enough, at his next lesson, he had already mastered the first line of the Gershwin piece, complete with his own creative fingering. Together, we worked through the entire piece over time while he diligently kept up with his other assignments. This pattern continued for many years. Eric's extraordinary talent and determination made teaching him a true joy.

Eventually, Eric waited out the year and rejoined the band, quickly becoming an outstanding member and a favorite in our community. His performances are always well-attended, and he is deeply respected by people in our community. After graduating from the University of Washington, where he continued his musical studies, Eric moved to New

York to pursue a career. As the song goes, "If you can make it there, you'll make it anywhere." It's so true.

Eric's success was also supported by his incredible parents, who not only encouraged him but were instrumental in helping me produce concerts he participated in. Teaching Eric was a deeply rewarding and meaningful experience in my teaching career.

The notes I've included above were written to me in a scrapbook that I kept for my students to write in during our piano parties. Over the years, I've taught more than 1,200 students and continue to teach today. It was impossible to include every story in this book, so I've highlighted a few that stood out as particularly memorable. That said, there are many other students whose stories and successes are equally remarkable.

One such student is Mira, who studied with me for several years. A brilliant pianist with exceptional talent and determination, Mira went on to graduate from the Juilliard School of Music in New York City, where she pursued her passion for violin. Thanks to her strong piano foundation, she was able to bypass Juilliard's two-year piano proficiency requirement, allowing her to focus on violin performance and composition. Mira aspires to become an orchestral conductor—a role that has historically been incredibly rare and challenging for women to attain. Despite the obstacles, I have no doubt that Mira will continue to strive with unwavering determination. With her remarkable talent, education, and drive, I fully expect to see her name among the few women who have broken through in this prestigious and demanding field.

Music Education for Children and Adults

Studying music offers profound benefits for both children and adults. For children, studying music helps to develop the skills of Creativity and Innovation, encouraging them to think outside the box, experiment with sounds, and to create something unique. Improvisation, composing, and interpreting pieces all stimulate creativity and problem-solving skills. Creativity and innovation are essential skills for the future. In an increasingly fast-paced and ever-changing world, children who can approach challenges creatively and adaptively are better equipped to succeed. These skills translate to all areas of life, from academic problem-solving to entrepreneurial thinking.

Music students learn how to embrace change, adapt to new techniques, and think critically. As industries shift and new technologies emerge, the ability to adapt quickly is invaluable.

Skills such as collaboration (from playing in ensembles), effective communication, and the self-discipline required to practice and master an instrument mirror the demands of real-world work environments.

Performing music teaches children to face challenges, overcome stage fright, and present themselves with poise. These experiences instill confidence in their abilities, helping them tackle public speaking, interviews, and other high-pressure situations in the future.

Success in mastering an instrument reinforces a growth mindset-the belief that hard work and persistence lead to improvement. This lesson carries over into all aspects of life, empowering children to tackle challenges with determination.

Studies show that music education enhances brain development in areas responsible for language, mathematics, and spacial reasoning. Spacial reasoning includes visualizing how objects fit together, imagining how they might look if rotated or flipped, and figuring out how to navigate through a space. It's the skill that helps us read maps, design structures, solve puzzles, and even pack a suitcase efficiently!. all while enjoying the process and watching their abilities grow with each challenge they tackle.

Engaging in music as an adult has been shown to improve cognitive function, delay cognitive decline, reduce the risk of dementia, and promotes brain health and lifelong learning. Learning an instrument keeps the brain sharp and healthy.

Playing music can be a wonderful outlet for children and adults to manage stress, process emotions, and find joy in creativity. It promotes the brain's ability to form new connections, which enhances specific cognitive abilities and makes individuals more capable, creative, and adaptable!

Playing music promotes mindfulness, fostering overall well-being. Sharing music with friends and family or participating in community performances brings connection and a sense of belonging. It provides an opportunity to express oneself, communicate emotions, and tell stories in ways that words cannot.

Learning music offers a sense of purpose, achievement, and joy, no matter a person's age or skill level. It teaches patience and the value of consistent effort.

Whether it's the thrill of mastering a challenging piece or the simple pleasure of playing for oneself, music is a source of immense joy.

Music lessons are far more than learning to play an instrument. It's a pathway to creativity, innovation, emotional depth, and lifelong growth-helping children prepare for their future and providing adults with the tools to lead vibrant, fulfilling lives. Whether at the beginning of life or later in adulthood, music offers gifts that enrich the mind, spirit, and community.

As I move forward in life, my mission is to champion music education and wellness for children, understanding that studying music enriches every aspect of their development. I encourage you, dear reader, to embrace music for yourself and your children, knowing that its power to inspire creativity, foster connection, and nurture the soul can help create a better and more beautiful world for us all.

About The Author

Maureen Girard was born and raised in the New York metropolitan area. She is an alumna of Willamette University in Salem, Oregon, where she was awarded a talent-based scholarship and completed studies in both classical and jazz piano. She also earned a two-year business degree from Merritt Davis Business College in Salem.

A dedicated music educator and leader, Maureen served as president of the local chapter of the Washington State Music Teachers Association and later founded the Washington State Association of Jazz Educators, a nonprofit established in 2004. She was the first performer to take the stage at the Whidbey Island Center for the Arts, opening for Grammy-winning jazz vocalist Diane Schuur at the venue's gala debut. Her own show, *The 88 Keys Piano Club*—named after her private studio—was later produced there. Over the years, Maureen has taught more than 1,200 students, including the grandson of the late Steve Allen, the original host of *The Tonight Show*. Her student won first place at the Lionel Hampton Jazz Festival, performing an arrangement written by Maureen. Today, Maureen is dedicated to championing music education and wellness for children, believing that music not only enriches lives but also shapes futures. Her memoir, **The Arctic Sonata: The Courage to Rise**, offers inspiration and encouragement for readers to overcome obstacles, embrace creativity, and follow their passions.

In the picture: Ray and the Author.

Photograph Credits

Photographs and Illustrations Courtesy Of:

The Lynch Family and Maureen Girard Private Collection

Minsky's Burlesque Records, 1922-1978. MS-00290. Special Collections and Archives, University Libraries, University of Nevada, Las Vegas. Las Vegas, Nevada.

National Maritime Museum/Public Domain: Artist John Wilson Carmichael's 1847 rendering of the HMS Erebus and HMS Terror in the High Arctic

Willamette University: Concert brochure

Society Expeditions: Map from Expedition Notebook detailing the proposed route